SUMMER COCKTAILS

"One martini is all right.
Two are too many,
and three are not enough."

—JAMES THURBER

❧

Library of Congress Cataloging in Publication Number: 2014944415

ISBN: 978-1-59474-785-4

Printed in China
Designed by Amanda Richmond
Production management by John J. McGurk

Photography and art direction by Tara Striano
Food styling and art direction by María del Mar Sacasa
Author portrait by Benoit Mouthon
Prop styling by Penelope Bouklas and Emily Rickard

Quirk Books
215 Church Street
Philadelphia, PA 19106
quirkbooks.com

10 9 8 7 6 5 4 3 2 1

SUMMER COCKTAILS

Margaritas, Mint Juleps, Punches, Party Snacks, and More

BY MARÍA DEL MAR SACASA

PHOTOGRAPHS BY TARA STRIANO

QUIRK BOOKS
PHILADELPHIA

CONTENTS

Introduction . . . 7

CLASSICS, THROWBACKS, AND NEW WAVE . . . 20

PUNCHES AND PITCHERS . . . 60

FROSTY DRINKS . . . 78

ANTIDOTES . . . 104

UNDERPINNINGS . . . 120

FILL YOUR PLATE . . . 132

Sources . . . 154

Index . . . 155

Acknowledgments . . . 159

About the Author and
  Photographer . . . 160

INTRODUCTION

HAMMOCKS, ROOFTOP PARTIES, PICNICS, BEACHES, LAKES, MOUNTAINS. Bikinis and the smell of sunscreen, sand in unmentionable places, porches and rocking chairs, the sun, the salt, the sweat. Even for those who live in latitudes where the sun shines year-round, *summer* is a special word, conjuring youth in all its lightheartedness, troubles shrugged off a freckled, golden shoulder.

This book is a companion for the golden season, with recipes ranging from classic to newfangled. It is separated into sections so that you may drink your way through old-school cocktails, brain-freezing slushy sips, potent punches, novel potions, and, in case you need reviving after all that, antidotes. But because ice and olives can't always be considered dinner, you can find recipes for real food tucked in the back.

A serious attitude is often taken in the field of mixology, and although it is indeed a craft, I'd like to invite you to approach this book casually, with thirst and curiosity. Read the recipes, get to know the spirits. Taste, experiment, and enjoy. *¡Salud!*

PANTRY AND FRIDGE BASICS

ONCE YOU'VE TASTED YOUR WAY THROUGH THIS BOOK, YOU'LL FIND COCKTAILS YOU come back to time and again, so always keep their components on hand. Here is a list of basics to help you begin shaking and stirring.

Bacon: Select high-quality, thick-cut bacon for more flavor and a deeply satisfying bite that is meaty and crunchy. For minimal mess, microwave bacon between layers of paper towels for about 6 minutes. Note that this method leaves you without fat that could be used for cooking. If using an oven, set an oven-safe cooling rack on a rimmed baking sheet, lay bacon across the rack, and bake on the middle rack in a preheated 375°F oven for about 12 minutes. If cooking on the stove, use a large skillet and don't overcrowd the bacon.

Chiles: Fresh chiles, like the jalapeño and its extra-hot cousin the serrano, are used to flavor and layer subtle heat in light summer drinks like the Green Goddess (page 94). Look for firm, smooth-skinned chiles. If you seek a milder burn, remove and discard the seeds and ribs. Morita chiles—smoked and dried jalapeños—are used in several recipes in this book, most notably to infuse Chiquila (page 129). Their heat is earthy and rich and pairs wondrously with summer fruits. Moritas are available in the Latin American section of most supermarkets.

Chocolate: I always use bittersweet chocolate in my recipes and for snacking, preferring the more intense flavor to that of milk chocolate. Look for varieties, either in bars or chips, that have 60 to 70 percent cacao content.

Club soda: This neutral, sparkling drink adds fizz and balances strong spirits without disturbing their flavors. Unless you plan to use a lot at once, keep small bottles on hand in the fridge, so you can add a splash here and there while preserving the carbonation.

Coconut milk (unsweetened): This popular alternative to dairy is used repeatedly throughout this book to flavor recipes like the Hot Watermelon Sherbet (page 93) and Piña Colada (page 82). Cream of coconut, the unctuous and sweetened blend frequently used in cocktails, is not recommended as a substitute; it overpowers otherwise balanced drinks.

Coffee: To get more out of it than just a caffeine boost, coffee should be carefully prepared and enjoyed. Use your favorite blend and, if possible, grind your beans for the freshest flavor. (A spice mill is perfect for small quantities.) French coffee presses, stovetop espresso makers, and regular coffee pots are all acceptable for making coffee. Always brew coffee right before using it.

Cola: I always opt for classic Coca-Cola, but use your favorite brand in drinks like the Cuba Libre (page 24). Always keep it well chilled.

Dried edible flowers: Dried lavender flowers and rosebuds lend their fragrance to the elegant Lazarus and Rosita wine spritzers (page 51). They are sometimes available at supermarkets; see Sources (page 154) for additional shopping suggestions.

Fresh herbs: Basil, cilantro, and mint are used frequently throughout this book. To clean herbs, fill a large bowl with cold water and soak for 1 to 2 minutes. Drain and repeat until the bottom of the bowl is free of sediment. Use herbs immediately or wrap leftovers in damp paper towels, place them in a plastic zip-top bag, and store in the refrigerator's crisper drawer.

Fresh produce: Many of these recipes rely on seasonal produce. Peaches, plums, rhubarb, and berries are available at supermarkets and farmers' markets. Eat locally and savor summer by taking advantage of what's ripe, juicy, and fragrant. Infuse liquors, make quick pickles, and invent new shrubs to preserve produce and use it in cocktails and other recipes year-round.

Fruit juices: The need for the freshest fruit juices in these cocktail recipes cannot be stressed enough. For tropical fruit nectars, such as passion fruit and guava, read the ingredients lists and avoid brands that are packed with additives and thickeners. Opt for reduced-sodium tomato juice whenever possible.

Ginger beer: Ginger ale is one of the most refreshing carbonated beverages I know, and I love the variety of craft versions, like Boylan's, that are available. However, I prefer the sharper taste of ginger beer, whose more aggressive flavor is a sharp and welcome addition to cocktails such as the Shandy (page 108) and the Dark and Stormy (page 46).

Honey: Honey is a natural sweetener and a favorite in this book, especially in syrup form (page 124). I prefer dark and raw varieties, as well as clover and orange blossom, but use your favorite. Pungent buckwheat honey is not for everyone, but its robustness is well suited to Chile-Spiced Honey Syrup (page 124).

Horseradish root: Look for this large root in the produce aisle, and ask for it if you don't spot it immediately, since it is sometimes hidden. Horseradish should be finely grated for cocktails, right before use because it oxidizes quickly. Prepared horseradish is available in the refrigerated section of the supermarket, but it is lackluster and missing the sharp, mustardlike burn of the fresh version.

Salt: Kosher salt is the go-to in these recipes, but Maldon sea salt, which has large, flat crystals, is called on for garnishes. It melts slowly and evenly into warm foods and drinks and also provides a pleasant crunch. For rimming glasses, use kosher salt or crush Maldon crystals with your fingers. Smoked salts, pink salts, and all their esoteric relatives can be used in lieu of the basic varieties as long as they are coarse.

Spices: Spices such as whole cloves, whole allspice, cinnamon sticks, black peppercorns, and coriander are crucial components of recipes like pickles and infused liquors. Spices lose potency with age, especially when stored in spaces that are constantly exposed to heat, such as cabinets above stovetops. Keep spices in a cool, dry area and avoid buying them in bulk so they don't go to waste. Many of the recipes in this book call for toasting whole spices in a dry skillet; this releases their flavor and fragrance and makes them more discernible. Dry spices are often "bloomed," that is, briefly cooked in fat, to achieve the same effect. Most of the spices called for here are available at general supermarkets, but see Sources (page 154) for harder-to-find items.

Sugar: Granulated, demerara, palm, and dark brown sugar are used in everything from flavored glass rims to syrups. Granulated sugar can be substituted in many cases. Read the recipe notes in this book to understand why some types of sugar are called for specifically.

Sweetened condensed milk: You should always have this sweet treat in your pantry. It takes care of a quick sugar fix, can be used to sweeten iced coffee or tea, and is a delicious alternative to chocolate syrup on a sundae. Keep it on hand for cocktails like the Piña Colada (page 82).

Tea: I like to make strong brews for my tea-based drinks, so the recipes call for specific ratios of tea to water, but feel free to adjust them as you please.

Tonic water: This carbonated drink contains quinine and is a staple at any bar. Keep small bottles in the refrigerator for such classics as the gin and tonic. Look for brands that contain more quinine for authentic flavor, which will produce a more polished drink.

Vinegar: This ingredient is a staple in pickle and shrub recipes, which abound in this book; keep an assortment in your pantry so that you can try as many as you like, and then experiment with your own mixes. Balsamic, red wine, cider, and white balsamic vinegars are among the types called for.

A GUIDE TO TOOLS AND SERVEWARE

MAKING A COCKTAIL CAN BE AS EASY AS POURING LIQUOR INTO A CLEAN GLASS (think whiskey neat), but for more elaborate mixes, a few tools are necessary. Following is a guide to tools and serveware that prove useful in cocktail making.

Baking pans: A 13-by-9-inch baking pan is very useful for making granitas (page 81).

Bar rags: Clean towels are perfect for cleaning up spills.

Blender and food processor: These appliances are time savers for pureeing fruits, whipping up ice pops, and preparing blended drinks like the Piña Colada (page 82) and the Peach Melba Shake (page 97). Powerful high-end blenders can adeptly break down many ingredients; if yours gets clogged or jammed, try cutting fruit into pieces smaller than the recipe recommends. Food processors are useful as well but should not be used when a blender is called for; their lower capacity may cause ingredients to overflow.

Bottle openers: Keep these on hand for popping open bottles of beer and carbonated beverages.

Cocktail napkins: Whether fabric or paper, these come in every color of the rainbow and are meant to keep your hands dry while drinking from a cold, wet glass.

Corkscrew: Although some wine bottles have screw tops, many a cork remains to be pulled.

Cutting boards: A small board is ideal for slicing citrus, chopping herbs, and prepping other ingredients and garnishes.

Fine-mesh sieve: For recipes that require ingredients to be strained, a fine-mesh sieve works best.

Ice bowl or bucket and tongs: Although not necessary, these two items add a nice touch to a bar.

Ice pick: Use it to break up large pieces of ice into shards and chunks.

Ice trays and molds: The most important underpinning in this book is ice. Small pieces melt easily and water down drinks: take the time to stock your freezer with homemade ice. Buy molds that make large cubes and orbs—especially when the weather is warm and your hot hand is wrapped around your cocktail (see page 154 for Sources). For punches and pitchers, go Goliath-size and make ice molds.

Jigger: If you want to mix your drinks properly, use a measure. Traditionally, a jigger is made of stainless steel and has an hourglass shape, with two different chambers for measuring liquids.

Knives: For chopping and dicing, an all-purpose chef's knife is necessary. A paring knife is good to have on hand, too, to cut lime wedges and other garnishes.

Metal mixing bowls or Bundt pans: Use Bundt pans or large metal mixing bowls to make ice molds for punches and pitchers. Larger pieces of ice are highly recommended for punches; the intent is to chill the punch but not water it down. You can also add visual interest to your molds by adding berries or other colorful fruits along with the water before freezing. To make a mold, start by filling a Bundt pan or medium-sized metal mixing bowl with water and freeze until set. To unmold, run the container under warm water, just until the ice begins to loosen. Turn the bowl over onto a clean kitchen towel to grip the container and lift it off the molded ice. Place the molded ice into your punch bowl or other serving vessel as directed by the recipe.

Muddler: This tool for smashing ingredients like fresh herbs, ginger, and sugar is often shaped like a baseball bat and has a fairly

ergonomic design. In a pinch, substitute a wooden spoon.

Pitchers: Have at least two on hand for making and serving punches, lemonades, and other drinks that are meant to serve a crowd. Glass vessels are most attractive, but plastic pitchers are well suited for casual gatherings and outdoor events.

Punch bowls: The punches in this book all yield about 96 ounces. A punch bowl is an ideal serving vessel, but if you don't own one, use another large vessel. Salad bowls, large pots, and pitchers are all good options.

Reamer or citrus juicer: These are efficient tools for getting the most juice from citrus fruits. They are conical, with a pointy end and sharply grooved sides. If you don't have either, use a fork.

Saucepans, large pots, and small skillets: Basic cookware is called for throughout this book for making syrups (pages 123–125) and pickles (pages 17 and 135) and to toast spices (page 129).

Shakers: There are three main types of cocktail shakers. All shakers are interchangeable; the type used is mostly a matter of preference. The Boston shaker consists of two parts: one stainless-steel cup and one glass or plastic pint cup. Ingredients are placed in the stainless-steel cup and the other is fitted over it prior to shaking. The cobbler shaker has three pieces: a stainless-steel cup, a built-in strainer, and a lid. The French shaker is a two-piece construction with a metal bottom and cap; a strainer is needed for serving. If you don't have any of these tools, you can shake cocktail ingredients together in a mason jar with a lid.

Stirrers or swizzle sticks: These long-necked spoons are useful for blending drinks in tall glasses.

Strainer: Bar strainers are small and fit the mouths of shaker cups. Several chilled drinks in this book contain ingredients and ice that need to be strained and discarded prior to pouring and serving. Larger strainers, cheesecloth, and reusable nut milk bags are useful for straining pulpy juices.

Zester: A fine zester is indispensable for creating garnishes and prepping the flavorful exterior of citrus fruits for use in recipes.

KNOW YOUR GLASSWARE

MAKING COCKTAILS IS INDEED A CRAFT, AND THERE ARE REASONS WHY SOME ARE served in very specific glasses. While I appreciate and often follow the rules and niceties, the lack of a perfect vessel will not prevent me from enjoying a drink. Use what you like, but pay attention to volume capacity and chilling instructions.

 Champagne glasses: Narrow flutes are slim and tall and allow you to see the characteristic bubbles of sparkling wine. Marie Antoinette–style or birdbath-style glasses, also known as coupes or champagne saucers, have wide, shallow bowls sitting atop slim stems.

 Cocktail or martini glasses: These have thin stems with conical bowls. Modern versions are sometimes available stemless.

 Collins glasses: Tall and slim, these glasses usually hold 10 to 12 ounces.

 Highball glasses: These tall glass tumblers are somewhat wider and a bit shorter than collins glasses. Capacity is normally 8 to 12 ounces.

 Old-fashioned glasses: Also known as lowball or rocks glasses, these short, stout, thick-based tumblers hold 5 to 10 ounces.

 Shot glasses: These short, footless glasses typically hold 1 1/2 ounces, though some are available in 1- or 2-ounce capacities. They are ideal for shooting spirits or, in a bind, good for measuring liquid ingredients for cocktails.

 Wine glasses: These come in different stem heights and bowl sizes and shapes; each is specific to the type of wine being served. They are a great serving option for a number of cocktails in this book, such as the Lazarus (page 51) and the Glinda (page 81).

THE WELL-STOCKED BAR

I USED TO DRINK ONLY WHAT WAS FAMILIAR: GIN, BOURBON OR RYE, WINE, AND beer. However, when I started creating drinks of my own, I found an abundance of spirits that captured my palate and imagination. Some of the results are gathered in this book. The next time you're at a bar or liquor store, don't be shy: ask for sample tastes and develop your palate. I'm not suggesting that you should own every item on this list; buy small bottles when possible, and stock your bar with your favorites so you'll be prepared for a thirsty evening or a casual drink with company.

Amaretto: This sweet almond-flavored liqueur is frequently served after dinner or combined with sour mix (page 131). It blends seamlessly into the Peachy Keen Punch (page 74) and highlights peaches in their peak.

Aperol: An Italian *aperitivo* that is bright reddish orange and bittersweet, this is a blend of bitter orange, herbs, and spices that is commonly used in a spritzer containing prosecco and club soda.

Asti Spumante: This Italian sparkling white wine made from Moscato grapes is called for in certain recipes to balance bitter spirits or citrus juices.

Bährenjäger: This German honey liqueur is based on neutral spirits, frequently vodka. A small amount imbues drinks like the Bee Sting (page 23) with intense honey flavor.

Beer: Bottled, canned, on draft—we all know beer. Varieties range from hopped-up IPAs to hefty dark brown stouts and seasonal craft beers flavored with spices. Beer's taste and consistency can dramatically vary. In this book they're the backbone or sidekick of two Antidotes (pages 108 and 114).

Bitters: Bitters are alcohols infused with herbs, roots, citrus peels, seeds, flowers, or fruits, from the most recognizable Angostura to specialty versions like plum and cherry. Bitters are added in dashes because their flavor is concentrated. Think of them as the salt that's added in pinches at the end of a recipe to adjust seasoning.

Bourbon: An American whiskey, bourbon is distilled from a blend of grains that must contain no less than 51 percent corn, which provides the characteristic sweetness. The remaining ingredients are usually barley, wheat, rye, or a combination thereof. The spirit is aged in flamed oak barrels, which lend it a smoky, easily recognizable flavor. This is a very potent potable: 80 percent alcohol by volume.

Brandy: This spirit is distilled from wine. Note that cognac is a type of brandy (it's named for the region of France in which it is produced), but not all brandy is cognac.

Campari: Like Aperol, Campari is a bitter *aperitivo* that I consider a must-have at any bar. Campari and soda over ice is ideal to begin a meal; the bitter taste will make you salivate and get your stomach rumbling. In this book it is used to cut through sweet sippers, such as Whitney's Lollipop (page 23).

Chambord: This French raspberry liqueur is known by its round, gold-capped bottle and pigeon's blood hue. Because it is syrupy and rich, a delicate pour is enough to flavor drinks like the Playa (page 27).

Champagne: Sparkling white wine can be called Champagne only if the grapes were grown in that region of France. Always chill Champagne prior to serving, either in a bucket of ice water for 30 to 45 minutes or in the refrigerator for 2 hours. Use a stopper to save leftovers for up to a week. Other sparkling wines are acceptable substitutes in recipes that call for Champagne; be sure to use the variety (sweet or dry) that the recipe calls for.

Chartreuse: This French liqueur is a furious shade of neon green mixed with violent yellow. It adds stringent and spiced sweetness to cocktails like the Nigel Barker (page 46).

Cocchi Americano: A white wine *aperitivo* from the Asti region of Italy, it is often used in cocktails in lieu of Lillet Blanc. You can drink it on the rocks as a simple cocktail, or add it to a number of cocktails, such as Queen of Hearts (page 48).

Crème de cassis: This is a black currant liqueur with a base of grape brandy or a neutral spirit. Sweet and deep red, it adds a velvety underpinning to drinks such as the Peach Melba Shake (page 97).

Domaine de Canton: This liqueur is sharply flavored with fresh ginger and makes drinks pop, as in Rainbow Sherbet Punch (page 68). Add a splash to classic cocktails like bourbon and ginger beer to create a backdrop of complementary flavor.

Drambuie: This liqueur is made from malt whiskey and contains honey, herbs, and spices. Try it in the Sourpuss (page 45).

Gin: This rather neutral spirit is distilled from grain and several herbs and spices, particularly juniper berries. Make it your own by flavoring it with infusions (pages 128–130).

Kahlúa: This coffee-flavored rum liqueur adds concentrated flavor and a punch of alcohol to drinks and frosty desserts like Ahogado (page 88).

Lambrusco: A type of effervescent Italian red wine, this is meant to be drunk young and cool. Its dry sweetness pairs well with rich dishes and, of course, lays the foundation for Dolce Far Niente (page 63).

Lillet: This white wine– and fruit liqueur–based French aperitif is available in blanc (used in this book), rosé, and rouge varieties. Recall 007 and have it in a Vesper with gin and vodka, try it in a number of cocktails in this book, or sip it neat on a hot summer evening, chilled and preferably on ice.

Luxardo maraschino liqueur: This sour cherry liqueur is made from the Luxardo marasca cherry, a variety grown only in the Veneto region of Italy. Often referred to as maraschino liqueur, it should not be confused with syrupy maraschino cherries.

Pimm's: An English "fruit cup," or liqueur made of gin flavored with herbs, spices, and fruits, this summer staple is often combined with carbonated beverages such as soda and ginger ale, lemonade, and fresh fruit garnishes.

Prosecco: Like Champagne, prosecco is a sparkling white wine, except it hails from Italy rather than France. Keep bottles chilled for use in various punch recipes and drinks. Or enjoy it as a predinner drink, either plain or with a distinctive additive like St-Germain (see below).

Rum: Rum is made by boiling sugarcane to thick molasses, which is then distilled and fermented. Dark rums are aged in oak barrels. Their flavor is richer and more intense than those of light rums, which are not aged and thus are ideal for infusing.

Sake: A Japanese alcoholic beverage made from fermented rice, sake deserves as much study as wine. Taste it in cocktails like the Chino-Latino (page 34), or try infusing it (page 128).

St-Germain: This French liqueur made from elderflowers picked in the Alps is an unmistakable additive to cocktails. It is extremely floral, so a little goes a long way. But it keeps for ages, especially in the fridge. Use it to add a twist to simple aperitifs and for drinks like the Lucky Loser (page 54).

Tequila: This Mexican spirit is distilled from the blue agave plant, a succulent with fleshy, pointy leaves. The clear, young variety, known as white tequila, is often stirred into cocktails like the Margarita (page 56). Carefully aged versions, such as gold and *añejo* tequilas, are sipped straight. Tequila is complex and uniquely perfumed, but white varieties adapt well to flavoring agents like cilantro and chiles.

Vodka: The backbone of many cocktails in this book and beyond, this clear, practically odorless, clean-tasting Russian-born spirit was originally distilled from potatoes; today's varieties contain grains and sugars. Like gin, vodka is an ideal backdrop for infusions (pages 128–130).

SHUCKING OYSTERS

Oysters are alive: when you buy them or pick them out, their shells should be tightly shut. Tap any that are slightly ajar, and if they don't close, discard them. Store oysters in the refrigerator in a container covered with a damp towel for up to 5 days. Do not cover them with plastic or anything that will deprive them of oxygen. Use only an oyster knife to shuck oysters.

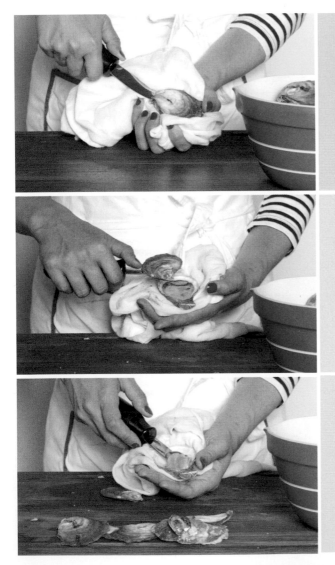

STEP 1: Scrub the oysters clean with a brush and water. Grasp one oyster, rounded side down, in a dishrag or place it on top of a dishrag on top a cutting board. Pry the tip of the oyster knife into the hinge, where the narrowest parts of the shells meet. You'll feel and hear a pop.

STEP 2: Slide the edge of the knife between the top and bottom shells, and then slide it straight across the top shell to separate the flesh.

STEP 3: Remove and discard the top shell, running the knife along the bottom of the oyster to separate it. Try to reserve as much of the liquid (known as "liquor") as possible. Arrange shucked oysters on a platter with crushed ice or seaweed.

QUICK PICKLING

Pickling is a delicious though somewhat time- and labor-intensive method of extending the shelf life of fresh fruits and vegetables while imbuing them with deep flavor. When you're pressed for time, this shortcut is the way to go. See pages 135—137 for specific recipes.

STEP 1: Toast spices in a dry skillet and then add the recipe's remaining ingredients and bring to a boil.

STEP 2: Meanwhile, prep vegetables (peel, trim, etc.) and cut them small enough to fit in a clean mason jar with a lid. Pack them into the jar.

STEP 3: Use a measuring cup with a spout or a funnel to transfer the pickling liquid to the jar. Refrigerate the pickles, uncovered, until completely chilled. Use immediately or cover and store for up to 5 days.

LEMONGRASS PREP

Lemongrass is a fragrant plant whose stalks are used in cooking and in the making of beauty, health, and lifestyle products. You may notice its citrusy scent in curries, soups, teas, and cocktails such as the Basilica (page 73) and the Ginger-Lemongrass Piña Colada (page 82). Look for lemongrass in the produce section of your supermarket: choose stalks that are firm and pale green and that do not appear dry or brittle.

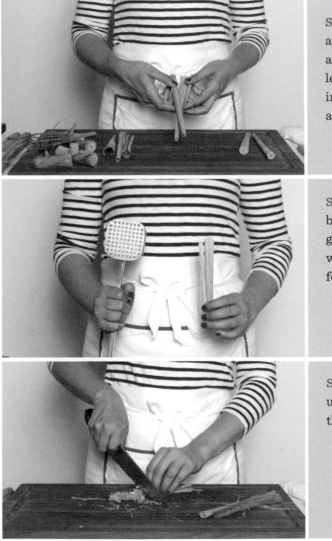

STEP 1: Using a sharp chef's knife, trim and discard the ends of the stalk. Peel and discard the outer layers until you are left with only the tender bulb. If not using immediately, wrap tightly in plastic wrap and freeze until ready to use.

STEP 2: The lemongrass is now ready to be prepared as is called for by the recipe: grate, thinly slice, chop, pound (such as with a meat tenderizer), or process in the food processor.

STEP 3: When chopping lemongrass, use a sharp knife that can cut through the extremely fibrous stalk.

PINEAPPLE PREP

Pineapples are much easier to break down than their prickly appearance lets on, and preparing the fruit yourself is more affordable than purchasing it already cubed. The core and skin are inedible but can be reserved and used as flavoring agents in recipes like Fresco de Arroz con Piña (page 34).

STEP 1: Scrub the pineapple with water and a brush. Lay it on its side on a cutting board and slice off the crown and the base.

STEP 2: Stand the pineapple upright and cut off the sides, cutting as far in as necessary to reveal the flesh. Reserve the trimmings for another recipe, if desired.

STEP 3: Run the knife parallel to the core to separate the core from the edible fruit, reserving core for another recipe if desired. Cut the fruit according to the recipe.

CLASSICS, THROWBACKS, and NEW WAVE

Several traditional cocktails have stood the test of time and can be requested at a bar by name: Martini! Greyhound! Manhattan! Warm-weather versions of many of these unique and trustworthy classics make an appearance in the following pages. Nostalgic drinks that hearken back to long-ago summers are included, as are novel potions that flirt with the old guard.

SHIRLEY TEMPLE . . . 23
Whitney's Lollipop . . . 23
BEE STING . . . 23
CUBA LIBRE . . . 24
Rum and Soda . . . 24
Cherry Pop . . . 24
Piscola . . . 24
KENTUCKY MULE . . . 26
Moscow Mule . . . 26
THE PLAYA . . . 27
Sex on the Beach . . . 27
LONG ISLAND ICED TEA . . . 29
PULPARINDO . . . 30
Piñata . . . 31
MINT JULEP . . . 32
South of the Border . . . 32
FRESCO DE ARROZ CON PIÑA . . . 34
CHINO-LATINO . . . 34
Arroz con Mango . . . 34
MARTINI . . . 37
As You Like It . . . 37
Flavor Flav . . . 37
The Marimar . . . 37
GIBSON . . . 39
DAIQUIRÍ . . . 40
El Papa Doble . . . 40
The Bumby . . . 40
THE BADDA BING . . . 40
Badda Bang! . . . 40
SHRUB COCKTAILS . . . 43

The Revolver . . . 43
The Poison . . . 43
In the Parlor . . . 43
Professor Plum . . . 44
The Butler . . . 44
The Dagger . . . 44
HONEY BADGER . . . 45
SOURPUSS . . . 45
Amaretto Sour . . . 45
THE NIGEL BARKER . . . 46
Greyhound . . . 46
Italian Greyhound . . . 46
Salty Dog . . . 46
DARK AND STORMY . . . 46
QUEEN OF HEARTS . . . 48
NEGRONI . . . 49
Negroni Sbagliato . . . 49
Negroni Vampiro . . . 49
THE LAZARUS . . . 51
La Rosita . . . 51
La Vie en Rose . . . 51
SAKE TO ME . . . 52
PIMM'S EDITIONS . . . 54
Matchpoint . . . 54
Lucky Loser . . . 54
Love-Love . . . 55
MARGARITA . . . 56
Chiquila Mockingbird Margarita . . . 56
Bollywood Margarita . . . 56
TROUBLE IN PARADISI . . . 59

Shirley Temple

Bouncing curls and tapping feet—it's no surprise that this pink and bubbly mocktail bears the name of the iconic child star. A friend and fellow child at heart used to cozy up to bartenders at parties to get an extra splash of grenadine or a cherry. Her version, which is spiked, follows the original.

3 ounces ginger ale
3 ounces lemon-lime soda
Dash grenadine (or more to taste)
Ice cubes
Maraschino cherry, for garnish

Combine ginger ale, lemon-lime soda, and grenadine in an ice-filled glass and stir gently to combine. Garnish with cherry and serve.

YOUNG AT HEART

Whitney's Lollipop
Substitute **passion fruit juice** for the ginger ale and add **1 ½ ounces bourbon** and ½ **ounce Campari**. Proceed with recipe.

Bee Sting

Hand a glass of Champagne to a guest walking into your party, and the night will be off to a good start. If you feel like popping open a swank bottle of bubbles, feel free to do so for this cocktail; the honey liqueur will accentuate, rather than muddle, its flavor. More budget-friendly sparkling wines and prosesccos also work well.

2 ounces Bärenjäger honey liqueur
Champagne, prosecco, or sparkling wine, chilled, to top

Pour honey liqueur into a champagne flute or bird-bath. Top with Champagne. Serve.

Cuba Libre

· SERVES 1 ·

The rum and Coke cocktail is a staple at bars. In Nicaragua, where I am from, it is a go-to order, called *ron con Coca* and always prepared with locally produced Flor de Caña rum. It is customary to order *una media*, a half-liter of light or dark rum, and the setup is always the same: a tray arranged with glass bottles of Coca-Cola and club soda, a small ice bucket, lime wedges, and highball glasses meticulously wrapped in white paper napkins. Old school never goes out of style.

Ice cubes

2 ounces golden or dark rum

Juice of 1 lime (or more to taste), plus lime wedge for garnish

Coca-Cola, chilled, to top

Fill a highball glass with ice cubes. Pour in rum and lime juice and stir to combine. Top with Coca-Cola, garnish with lime wedge, and serve.

THE OTHER GO-TO

Rum and Soda

Substitute **chilled club soda** for Coca-Cola.

WITH A CHERRY ON TOP

Cherry Pop

Add **1 ounce Cherry-Vanilla Syrup** (page 125) in lieu of lime juice.

THE ANDEAN TIPPLER

Piscola

Substitute **pisco** for the rum.

Kentucky Mule

Quality ingredients are never more important than in recipes made with only a few of them. To make this mule from Kentucky, use your favorite bourbon, squeeze fresh citrus, and make a run to the market for ginger beer—its sharpness and fragrance make all the difference. For extra kick, slip in slices of fresh or candied ginger.

Ice cubes

2 ounces bourbon

Juice of 1 lime (or more to taste), plus lime wedge for garnish

Ginger beer, chilled, to top

Fresh ginger slices or candied ginger for garnish (optional)

Fill a highball glass with ice cubes. Pour in bourbon and lime juice and stir to combine. Top with ginger beer and garnish with lime wedge and fresh or candied ginger, if desired. Serve.

MULE-TY TALENTED

Moscow Mule

Substitute **2 ounces vodka** for the bourbon.

Sippy Cup

A mule is traditionally served in a copper mug. Though the clothes don't make the man, this traditional vessel adds a historical note and keeps the drink chilled.

The Playa

The classic Sex on the Beach is made with vodka, peach schnapps, orange or pineapple juice, and cranberry juice. This decidedly more sophisticated version relies on seasonal peaches, infused liquor, and bitter Campari.

1 peach, pitted and cubed, or ¾ cup frozen peaches

1½ ounces vodka, gin, or Pineapple Rum (page 130)

1½ ounces fresh orange juice or pineapple juice

1½ ounces Campari

½ ounce Chambord or crème de cassis

½ cup ice cubes

Maraschino cherries, orange wedges, or pineapples cubes, for garnish

In a blender, pulse peaches, spirit, juice, Campari, Chambord, and ice cubes until well blended. Garnish as desired and serve immediately.

A SHORE THING

Sex on the Beach

In a shaker, combine **1½ ounces vodka**, **1 ounce peach schnapps**, **1 ounce Chambord**, **2 ounces pineapple or orange juice**, and **1 ounce cranberry juice**. Add **a handful of ice cubes**, shake, and pour into an ice-filled glass. Garnish with **maraschino cherries**.

Long Island Iced Tea

· SERVES 1 ·

Admittedly, I haven't had much of this "tea" since I was a lot younger and sillier. But there is a time and a place for everything! If you need to feel young again (hangover included at no extra charge) or decide to fool around with your hotel minibar, this is the drink for you.

½ ounce gin

½ ounce light rum

½ ounce silver tequila

½ ounce triple sec or Cointreau

½ ounce vodka

½ ounce Homemade
   Sour Mix (page 131)

Ice cubes

Chilled cola, to top

Lime wedge, for garnish

Stir together gin, rum, tequila, triple sec, vodka, sour mix, and ice in a highball or collins glass. Top with chilled cola and garnish with lime wedge. Serve.

Pulparindo

· SERVES 1 ·

I spent a few years of my childhood in Mexico City and quickly grew to love the cuisine, which is complex and often loaded with heat. With time the burn became manageable, and soon I was sprinkling *chile pequín* powder on cucumber slices and jicama sticks doused with lime juice and salt. One of my favorite fruit-and-chile combinations was a tamarind fruit chew called Pulparindo—salty, sweet, tart, and spicy. This drink is based on my memories of Mexico.

1 tablespoon flaky sea salt or coarse salt

2 teaspoons ground chile pequín*

3 tablespoons Simple Syrup (page 123)

Ice cubes

2 teaspoons tamarind concentrate**

2 tablespoons water

1½ ounces Chiquila (page 129)

3 tablespoons fresh grapefruit juice

Grapefruit wedge, for garnish

Combine salt and chile pequín on a small plate or saucer. Pour 1 tablespoon of the simple syrup onto a second plate. Dip a chilled 1-cup-capacity glass into the syrup and then into the salt–pequín mixture to coat; shake off excess. Fill glass with ice.

Stir together tamarind concentrate and water in a shaker until dissolved. Add Chiquila, grapefruit juice, the remaining 2 tablespoons simple syrup, and a handful of ice. Shake vigorously and strain into prepared glass. Garnish with grapefruit wedge and serve.

A PINEAPPLE A DAY

Piñata
Substitute **fresh pineapple juice** for the grapefruit juice.

Pequín chiles are small but very spicy. For the rim in this drink, I like to use Pico de Gallo brand Pico Piquín seasoning, a blend of chile powder and salt. Dried pequín peppers can be used as well; simply crush and blend with salt. Both items can be found online or at Latin American markets.

**Tamarind is a tropical tree that produces firm brown pods with datelike flesh and large seeds. Its tart, sweet, and citrusy notes have made it a popular ingredient in Indian, Mexican, and Australian cuisines. The concentrate called for in this recipe is easy to use and available in specialty markets and online.

Mint Julep

SERVES 1

Spearmint, crushed ice, bourbon, frosty silver cups, and outlandish hats: the Mint Julep instantly conjures Southern comfort, charm, and civility. Tradition aside, it's also air-conditioning in a cup—easy bliss on a sweltering day.

1 ounce Simple Syrup (page 123)

8 to 10 spearmint leaves, plus a handful of mint sprigs for garnish*

2 cups crushed ice

2 ounces bourbon

Spearmint is a bit milder than peppermint. If you are using peppermint, avoid the larger leaves, which tend to be bitter.

Place simple syrup in a silver or pewter julep cup. Place a couple mint leaves in one hand and clap the other hand over them once or twice to release their oils. Rub the inside of the cup with the leaves and drop them into the cup. After you've added 8 to 10 mint leaves, lightly bruise leaves with a wooden muddler or spoon.

Fill cup halfway with ice, add bourbon, and stir until cup is frosted. Add more ice, gently stir, and top with a large bouquet of mint.

HORSING AROUND

South of the Border

Replace half of the mint leaves with **cilantro leaves** and use **dark rum or Ginger Rum** (page 130) instead of bourbon.

Keep Your Hands to Yourself

Part of the allure of a julep is the white layer of frost that forms on the outside of the cup. When preparing juleps, touch only the rim or the base of the glass to avoid leaving fingerprints. If you don't have julep cups, use highball glasses.

Fresco de Arroz con Piña

MAKES 2 QUARTS

This is a common drink in Nicaragua, where I am from. The texture is velvety and smooth. It's a soothing accompaniment to meals that are intensely spicy.

12 cups water

Rind and core of 1 scrubbed pineapple, cut into 3-inch pieces (see page 19)

1 cup long grain white rice

½ teaspoon salt

Finely grated zest of 1 orange

2 cups granulated sugar

1 teaspoon pure vanilla extract

Simple Syrup (page 123), to taste

In a large pot, bring water, pineapple rind and core, rice, and salt to a boil over medium-high heat. Reduce heat to medium and simmer until pineapple pieces are soft, 45 to 60 minutes. Rub orange zest into sugar until no strands remain, then add to pot and cook, stirring, until completely dissolved. Remove from heat and cool completely.

In a blender, pulse pineapple-rice mixture and strain into a pitcher. Discard solids. Add vanilla extract. Although this beverage is meant to be thick, like pear juice, you can stir in water to thin it as desired. Adjust sweetness with simple syrup to taste.

Refrigerate fresco until completely chilled before using. Fresco may be kept refrigerated for up to 3 days. Leftovers may be frozen for up to 1 month in sturdy zip-top bags; thaw prior to use.

Chino-Latino

SERVES 1

Chino-Latino is a term describing a cross-breed of cuisines that contains Asian and Latin American influences. Think roasted chicken marinated in soy sauce, mounds of white rice, crispy pork bits, fried sweet plantains, and charred corn tortillas. This drink toasts Chino-Latino cuisine by combining *fresco de arroz con piña* with sake, the fermented rice beverage. The silky result makes a great alternative to dessert.

4 ounces Fresco de Arroz con Piña (see left)

2 ounces dry sake

Ice cubes

Fresh pineapple cubes, for garnish

Combine fresco and sake in an ice-filled glass and stir to combine. (If you prefer a frosty drink, pulse ingredients together in a blender.) Garnish with pineapple cubes and serve.

FOR MANGO LOVERS

Arroz con Mango

Substitute **Ginger Rum** (page 130) for the sake and add **2 ounces mango nectar** and **1 ounce Mango Shrub** (page 127). Garnish with a **fresh mango wedge**.

Chino-Latino

Martini

There is much to be said about this elemental cocktail, but the most important is this: May I please have another? Though many argue over how dry, wet, or dirty they like their martini, I say drink and be merry. And drink more and be merrier with the following polished variations.

2½ ounces gin
½ ounce dry vermouth
Ice cubes
Olives or lemon twist, for garnish

Stir gin and vermouth together in a shaker or glass filled with ice for about 30 seconds. Strain into a chilled martini glass. Garnish with olives or lemon twist. Serve.

HIGH AND DRY
As You Like It

A dry martini (as above) has a small amount of dry vermouth, whereas a wet martini has much more. Extra-dry has even less vermouth—often just enough to rinse the glass—or none at all. Dirty martinis are muddied with olive brine, and perfect martinis contain equal amounts of sweet and dry vermouth.

SUMMER GARDEN VARIATIONS
Flavor Flav

Substitute **Dill, Cucumber, and Black Peppercorn Gin or Vodka** (page 129) for the gin and garnish with **1 Persian cucumber slice** and **1 dill sprig**. Alternatively, replace gin with **Shiso and Shishito Pepper Gin or Vodka** (page 130), garnish with **1 shiso leaf**, and serve with **Charred Shishito Peppers** (page 141). You can also try a martini made with **Rhubarb and Celery Gin or Vodka** (page 129) and garnished with a **celery stick** or **sliced strawberry**.

YOUR WORD IS YOUR BOND
The Marimar

The Vesper, 007's signature order of gin, vodka, and Lillet Blanc, doffs a layer for this hot-weather healer. Combine **2 ounces gin** and **2 ounces Lillet Blanc** in an ice-filled lowball glass. Garnish with a **lemon twist**. Serve.

Flavor Flav garnished with a shiso leaf and served with Charred Shishito Peppers (page 141)

Gibson

SERVES 1

A Gibson is much the same as a martini but for the finishing touch—a cocktail onion instead of an olive or lemon twist. For an extra-swanky touch, accentuate your Gibson with homemade pickled vegetables (see page 17), like radishes, okra, and, of course, the classic onion.

2½ ounces gin
½ ounce dry vermouth
Ice cubes
Pickled onions, for garnish

Stir gin and vermouth together in a shaker or glass filled with ice for about 30 seconds. Strain into a chilled martini glass and garnish with onions. Serve.

Daiquirí
· SERVES 1 ·

Forget the fruity drinks the cabana boy hands you at the pool in a resort. The real daiquirí is spare and certain, like Ernest Hemingway's writing. Papa threw back these lime and light rum drinks, sometimes two at a time, with a special twist: grapefruit juice and maraschino liqueur were added to the mix. Go single or kick back and have a drink like Papa.

2 ounces light rum
¾ ounce fresh lime juice
½ ounce Simple Syrup (page 123)
Ice cubes
Lime slice, for garnish

Combine rum, lime juice, and syrup in an ice-filled shaker. Shake vigorously and strain into a chilled glass. Garnish with lime slice and serve.

DEUCES WILD
El Papa Doble

Add ½ **ounce fresh grapefruit juice** and ½ **ounce maraschino liqueur** to the shaker and proceed with recipe. If you have Hemingway's lust for liquor, add more rum. Garnish with a **grapefruit twist**.

THE HEART REMAINS A CHILD
The Bumby

Replace the rum with **Cocchi Americano** and add ½ **ounce Campari** to the shaker. Proceed with recipe. Pour drink into an ice-filled glass and top with **dry orange soda** (such as San Pellegrino). Garnish with an **orange twist**.

The Badda Bing
· SERVES 1 ·

Homemade cherry-vanilla syrup is the star of this old-school soda fountain throwback. The rye's smoky backbone balances perfectly with acidic lime juice and sharp ginger beer.

6 fresh cherries plus more for garnish, pitted*
2 ounces rye whiskey
1 ounce Cherry-Vanilla Syrup (page 125)
Crushed ice
Ginger beer, chilled, to top**

Place cherries in a shaker and smash with a muddler or the back of a wooden spoon. Add rye and syrup. Shake vigorously and pour into an ice-filled glass. Top with ginger beer, garnish with cherries, and serve.

A cherry pitter makes easy work of removing the inedible seeds. Give it a squeeze and pop!—out comes the pit. Alternatively, set cherries on a cutting board and press gently on each one with the flat side of a chef's knife; then remove the pit with your fingertips. Make sure you're wearing an apron or an old T-shirt because cherry juice stains.

**Ginger beer has a much more assertive flavor than ginger ale. Substituting the latter results in a meeker drink.*

A DRINK WITH PIZZAZZ
Badda Bang!

Replace rye with **bourbon** and add **2 teaspoons fresh lemon juice** to the shaker. Top with **chilled club soda** instead of ginger beer and garnish with **Pickled Cherries** (page 135).

Daiquirí (top) and the Bumby (bottom)

Shrub Cocktails

The shrub is an eye—and palate—opener. These vinegary additions will make any cocktail (or even mocktail) really sing. Bitters, aperitifs like Campari, and drying agents like white vermouth help even out sweet cocktails (similar to the way salt added to desserts takes them from flat to 3-D), but shrubs add a difficult-to-identify undercurrent that sweeps drinkers off their feet. An added bonus: you can use these fruity vinegars in salad dressings. See page 126 for how to make your own.

BAM!

The Revolver

In a shaker, stir together **2 ounces Blackberry-Basil Shrub** (page 127), **2 ounces gin**, ½ **ounce elderflower liqueur**, and **ice** for about 30 seconds. Strain into a chilled glass and top with **chilled club soda or prosecco**. Garnish with **blackberries** and **basil**, if desired.

IT GOES DOWN EASY

The Poison

Pour **1 ounce shrub of your choice** (pages 126–127) into a champagne flute or birdbath and top with **chilled Champagne or sparkling wine**, preferably sweet. If using Strawberry-Rosemary Shrub (page 127), add ½ ounce amaretto. Serve.

BEFORE-DINNER TREAT

In the Parlor

Stir **2 ounces Strawberry-Rosemary Shrub or other shrub of your choice** (pages 126–127), **3 ounces sweet vermouth**, and **ice cubes** in a shaker for about 30 seconds. Strain into a chilled glass and serve.

From left to right: In the Parlor,
the Revolver, Professor Plum, and the Butler

A RHUBARB-PLUM SHRUB COCKTAIL

Professor Plum

Stir **2 ounces bourbon**, **2 ounces Rhubarb-Plum Shrub** (page 127), and **ice cubes** in a shaker for about 30 seconds. Strain into an ice-filled glass and top with **chilled club soda or dry ginger ale**. Garnish with a **plum wedge**.

AS YOU LIKE IT

The Butler

Pour **1 ounce Raspberry Shrub or other berry shrub** (pages 126–127) and **1 ounce Blackberry Gin** (page 130) into a champagne flute or coupe. Top with **chilled demi-sec Champagne**.

TO THE POINT

The Dagger

Pour **2 ounces light rum** and **1 ounce Mango Shrub** (page 127) into an ice-filled glass and stir gently to combine. Top with **chilled club soda**.

Honey Badger

· SERVES 1 ·

While bubbles tickle the tongue, ruddy bourbon and spicy honey tease the throat and cause brows to dampen. The resulting cocktail is a coy mixture of naughty and nice.

2 ounces bourbon
2 tablespoons Chile-Spiced Honey Syrup (page 124)
2 teaspoons fresh lemon juice
Ice cubes
Chilled sparkling wine or Champagne*

Place bourbon, syrup, and lemon juice in a shaker filled with ice. Shake vigorously and strain into a chilled glass. Top with sparkling wine or Champagne and serve.

Avoid dry/brut bubbly here. In spite of the honey syrup, it will make the drink too harsh.

Sourpuss

· SERVES 1 ·

This libation, made with malt whiskey, honey, and herb liqueur, is a more cunning version of its fraternal twin, the amaretto sour.

2 ounces Drambuie
1 ounce Homemade Sour Mix (page 131)
Ice cubes
Splash Campari

Place Drambuie and sour mix in a shaker filled with ice. Shake vigorously and strain into an ice-filled glass. Top with Campari and serve.

THE GO-TO

Amaretto Sour
Substitute **amaretto or almond liqueur** for the Drambuie and omit the Campari. Garnish with **maraschino cherries** and serve with **smoked almonds.**

The Nigel Barker

SERVES 1

This graceful libation is inspired by the elegance and poise of an Italian greyhound of my acquaintance. The original Greyhound cocktail and its variations follow.

3 ounces fresh grapefruit juice
2 ounces Cocchi Americano
1½ ounces vodka
Splash Chartreuse
Ice cubes
Dash smoked sea salt

Place grapefruit juice, Cocchi Americano, vodka, and Chartreuse in a shaker with ice. Shake vigorously and strain into an ice-filled glass. Top with smoked sea salt and serve.

THE ORIGINAL

Greyhound

Place **2 ounces vodka** and **4 ounces fresh grapefruit juice** in a shaker with ice and shake vigorously. Strain into an ice-filled glass.

EVERY DOG HAS ITS DAY

Italian Greyhound

Add a **splash of Campari** to the Greyhound.

WORTH ITS SALT

Salty Dog

Serve the Greyhound in a **salt-rimmed glass**.

Dark and Stormy

SERVES 1

Pirates, sailors, the Caribbean—it's easy to get carried away with the notion of windy seas when enjoying this cocktail. Opt for the darkest of rums and the sharpest of ginger beers for a properly bracing beverage.

Ice cubes
2 to 3 slices fresh ginger*
2 ounces dark rum
4 to 6 ounces ginger beer
2 lime wedges

Fill a highball glass with ice cubes and ginger slices. Pour rum into prepared glass. Top with ginger beer, squeeze in one lime wedge, and garnish with the other. Serve.

Thinly slice ginger with a vegetable peeler.

Dark and Stormy

Queen of Hearts

An after-work cocktail at the local bar is fine, but sometimes a favorite chair, takeout, and an indulgent drink at home are the perfect prescription. This Dubonnet and Cocchi Americano option makes an elegant aperitif. If Dubonnet is good enough for the queen, it's good enough for you.

1½ ounces Dubonnet
1½ ounces Cocchi Americano
½ ounce Cointreau
Ice cubes
Orange twist, for garnish*

Release more natural oils, and hence more flavor, from citrus zest by rubbing it. Or let heat accentuate its fragrance: carefully run the flame of a lit match along an orange twist. Extinguish the match, rub zest along the glass rim, and place zest in cocktail.

Stir Dubonnet, Cocchi, and Cointreau together in an ice-filled lowball glass. Garnish with orange twist. Serve.

Negroni

· SERVES 1 ·

An aperitif is a cocktail served as a precursor to dinner. It should contain a bitter spirit, which causes the mouth to salivate and sharpens the appetite. This Italian Campari cocktail will definitely make your mouth water.

1 ounce gin

1 ounce Campari

1 ounce red vermouth

Ice (preferably large orbs or cubes)

Orange twist, for garnish

Stir gin, Campari, and vermouth in an ice-filled shaker. Strain into an ice-filled lowball glass and garnish with orange twist.

LUCKY MISTAKE

Negroni Sbagliato

Serve the Negroni in a coupe without ice and top with **brut Champagne**.

RED-BLOODED

Negroni Vampiro

Combine gin with **Lillet Blanc or Cocchi Americano**, omit the ice, and add just a drop each of **red vermouth** and **Campari**.

The Lazarus

• SERVES 1 •

As a regular drinker of straight gin, bourbon, and whiskey, I've never understood the hyper-diluted cocktail. The wine spritzer conjures images of Barbie in a '70s poly-blend housecoat with Muzak tinkling in the background. But this spritzer and its variations are delicate and sharp, pairing lavender and rose simple syrups with sharp wines and very little club soda. Save the spritz for the sprinkler system.

1 ounce Lavender Syrup
   (page 124)

4 ounces dry white wine, chilled

Club soda, chilled (optional)

Place syrup in a wine glass and add white wine. Top with a splash of club soda, if desired.

EVERY ROSE HAS ITS THORN

La Rosita

Replace the Lavender Syrup with **Rose Syrup** (page 124), add **¼ ounce Averna**, and use **brut pink Champagne or dry rosé** in lieu of white wine. The club soda topper is optional.

I LOVE PARIS

La Vie en Rose

Replace the white wine with **rosé or pink sparkling wine**. For an extra kick, add **2 ounces Black Peppercorn Gin or Vodka** (page 129).

The Lazarus (left) and La Rosita (right)

Sake to Me

Sake is the popular fermented rice drink (alcoholic, naturally) you're used to ordering at sushi restaurants. Make it fresh and fragrant by combining it with one of summer's favorite fruits: peaches.

2 ounces peach purée, chilled (see below)

2 ounces sake, chilled

Fresh peach wedge, for garnish (optional)

PEACH PURÉE

2 ripe peaches, pitted and cut into ½-inch cubes*

2 teaspoons freshly grated ginger

2 to 3 tablespoons water or Simple Syrup (page 123)

Pinch salt

Ice cubes

Clingstone peaches can be difficult to pit. Run a knife along the circumference of the peach and then twist and turn the halves until one come loose. Cut the remaining half into wedges and carefully pull them off the pit.

Stir together peach purée and sake and serve in a chilled glass. Garnish with peach wedge if desired.

To purée the peaches: Pulse peaches, ginger, water or simple syrup, and salt in a blender until smooth. Add ice cubes and pulse until mixture is broken down and has the texture of a smoothie. Makes 1 cup.

Pimm's Editions

Pimm's is a gin-based variety of a drink known in England as a fruit cup, that is to say, gin flavored with herbs and spices. The drink is synonymous with English summer, and it helps beat the heat.

2 ounces Pimm's No. 1

6 ounces fresh lemon juice sweetened with Simple Syrup (page 123) to taste

Ice cubes

Rosemary, thyme, mint leaves, orange slices, cucumber slices, and/or strawberry slices, for garnish

Combine Pimm's and sweetened lemon juice in an ice-filled shaker. Shake vigorously and pour into an ice-filled glass. Garnish as desired and serve.

A PROPER VARIATION

Matchpoint

Replace the sweetened lemon juice with **3 ounces guava juice** and **1 ounce Strawberry-Rosemary Shrub** (page 127). Proceed with recipe and garnish with **rosemary sprigs** and **strawberry slices**.

GINGERLY

Lucky Loser

Combine Pimm's and **1 ounce St-Germain elderflower liqueur** in an ice-filled shaker. Continue with recipe and top with **3 ounces chilled ginger beer**. Garnish with **thyme sprigs** and **fresh blackberries**.

IN YOUR COURT

Love-Love

Combine Pimm's and **1 ounce Strawberry Vodka** (page 130) in an ice-filled shaker. Continue with recipe and top with **3 ounces chilled lemon soda**. Garnish with **mint**.

How to Clean Herbs

Fill a large bowl with cold tap water, place a bunch of herbs in it, and shake them to release debris. Remove the herbs, drain and rinse the bowl, refill, and repeat the process until no sediment remains. Shake out the herbs or dry them in a salad spinner and store in zip-top plastic bags in the crisper drawer of the refrigerator.

Matchpoint (left) and Lucky Loser (right)

Margarita

· MAKES 1 ·

I hear that a kiss with a Latin accent makes its recipient weak in the knees. That may well be fiction, but this drink is guaranteed to make anyone swoon.

2 tablespoons kosher salt

½ lime

Ice

2 ounces tequila

1 ounce triple sec or Cointreau

1 ounce fresh lime juice or Lime Sour Mix (see page 131)

Spread salt on a small plate or saucer. Rub the rim of a glass with lime to moisten. Dip rim into salt and shake off excess. Fill glass with ice.

Combine tequila, triple sec, and lime juice in a shaker. Shake vigorously and strain into prepared glass. Serve.

THINGS THAT MAKE YOU GO ¡AY!

Chiquila Mockingbird Margarita

Replace tequila with **Chiquila** (page 129) and add **1 ounce Honey Syrup** (page 124) to the shaker. Continue with recipe.

MUMBAI MADNESS

Bollywood Margarita

Rim glass as in recipe. Place **6 toasted fresh curry leaves** in a cocktail shaker and crush them with a muddler or the back of a wooden spoon. Add **2 ounces Tomatillo and Coriander Tequila** (page 129), **1 ounce fresh lime juice**, and **1 ounce Honey Syrup** (page 124). Shake vigorously and strain into prepared glass.

Make it Yours

These recipes call for two of the infused tequilas in this book, but feel free to branch out and try new variations with your own infusions. See page 128 for how to make them.

Trouble in Paradisi

Citrus paradisi, known as "the forbidden fruit" or the more prosaic "grapefruit," is the headliner in this simple cocktail that will become essential to your arsenal. Aperol's bitter citrus and rhubarb undertones spark up the drink, and precipitous pisco takes it for a spin.

2 ounces pisco

1½ ounces Aperol

2 ounces fresh grapefruit juice

Ice

Grapefruit supreme or slice, for garnish

Place pisco, Aperol, and juice in a shaker filled with ice. Shake vigorously and strain into a chilled glass. Garnish with grapefruit and serve.

PUNCHES *and* PITCHERS

Punch is always welcome at a summer party.

It's refreshing, cooling, convivial, and a little bit dangerous.
Nothing says celebration like a large brimming bowl or
pitcher studded with fruit, ice, and fizz. Party on.

DOLCE FAR NIENTE . . . 63

LA DOLCE VITA . . . 64

LIMEADE . . . 66

Lavandula . . . 66

Bramble . . . 66

Cool as a Cucumber . . . 66

RAINBOW SHERBET PUNCH . . . 68

SUNNY SIDE UP PUNCH . . . 70

MOROCCAN MINT ICED TEA . . . 70

LEMONADE . . . 73

Basilica . . . 73

Raspberry Beret . . . 73

The Marty . . . 73

Pink Ladies Lemonade . . . 73

PEACHY KEEN PUNCH . . . 74

HAWAIIAN PUNCH . . . 77

TICKLED PINK PUNCH . . . 77

Dolce Far Niente

• MAKES ABOUT 13 CUPS (ABOUT 3 QUARTS), SERVES 24 •

Sangría is a traditional Spanish sweetened red wine named for its sanguine hue. This edition retains the drink's bleeding soul and traditional ingredients such as fresh juice, brandy, and summer stone fruits, but it is made with Lambrusco, a *frizzante* (lightly sparkling) red wine from the Emilia-Romagna region of Italy. Thyme and rosemary accentuate the fruit-forward spirit of this drink.

4 peaches, nectarines, plums, or a combination, pitted and cut into ½-inch cubes or wedges

2 teaspoons finely grated orange zest

1 tablespoon granulated sugar

2 cups brandy

2 (750-milliliter) bottles Lambrusco, chilled*

2 cups fresh orange juice, strained and chilled

2 cups club soda, chilled

1 cup Homemade Sour Mix (page 131)

Large ice pieces or cubes for punch, plus smaller pieces for serving

Fresh thyme and rosemary sprigs, for garnish

Lambrusco loses its fizz rather quickly, so don't expect it to come out of the bottle and behave as effervescently as Champagne.

Place fruit in a large bowl. Rub orange zest into sugar until no strands remain and then sprinkle the mixture over fruit. Add brandy. Let mixture rest at room temperature for 1 to 2 hours.

Stir together wine, orange juice, club soda, and sour mix in a punch or other serving bowl. Add several large pieces or cubes of ice and the fruit-brandy mixture, and stir. Serve drink in ice-filled cups or glasses, adding a scoop of fruit to each portion. Garnish with sprigs of fresh thyme and/or rosemary and serve immediately.

Let it Sit

Maceration is a process in which a fruit (fresh or dried) is soaked in a flavoring liquid, such as alcohol, to imbue it with flavor. Sprinkling sugar on fruit and letting it sit is also considered macerating, because the sugar draws out the fruits' juices. In this recipe, both citrus sugar and a spirit are used to macerate the fruit and spirits, adding brightness and marrying the ingredients' flavors.

La Dolce Vita

This sangría is made with Asti, a true sparkling wine. Produced in the region of Italy with the same name, Asti is made from sweet white Moscato grapes. This recipe balances the wine with tart, dry lemon soda and green apple pieces.

2 Granny Smith apples, cored and cut into ½-inch cubes

2 teaspoons finely grated lemon zest

1 tablespoon granulated sugar

2 cups brandy

1 tablespoon lemon juice

2 (750-milliliter) bottles Asti Spumante, chilled

2 cups fresh tangerine juice, strained and chilled

2 cups dry lemon soda, such as San Pellegrino brand, chilled

1 cup Homemade Sour Mix (page 131)

Large ice pieces or cubes

1 cup red and/or white grapes, thinly sliced

Fresh thyme and rosemary sprigs, for garnish

Place apples in a large bowl. Rub lemon zest into sugar until no strands remain and sprinkle mixture on apples. Add brandy and lemon juice. Let rest at room temperature for 1 to 2 hours.

Stir together wine, tangerine juice, lemon soda, and sour mix in a punch or other serving bowl. Add several large pieces or cubes of ice, the apple-brandy mixture, and grapes. Stir. Serve drink in ice-filled cups or glasses, adding a scoop of fruit to each. Garnish with sprigs of fresh thyme and/or rosemary and serve immediately.

Two sparkling sangrías: white La Dolce Vita and red Dolce Far Niente (page 63)

Limeade

• SERVES 1 •

Limes—tiny, emerald green, and tart enough to make you pucker your lips like a guppy—were flush where I grew up, and I think their sweetened, freshly squeezed juice is a hot day's most refreshing companion. Lemonade was a thing of fiction, for the sunny citrus were nonexistent in our latitude. This limeade and its variations are not overly sweetened, so you may want to serve them with syrup—simple or flavored—on the side.

2 ounces gin, vodka, white rum, pisco, or dry sake

¼ cup freshly squeezed lime juice

½ teaspoon finely grated lime zest

1 tablespoon Simple Syrup made with palm sugar (page 123; see ingredient note), or more to taste

Pinch salt

Ice cubes

¼ cup club soda, chilled

Lime rounds, for garnish (optional)

Stir together liquor, lime juice and zest, syrup, and salt in an ice-filled shaker for about 30 seconds. Add club soda and stir just to combine. Strain into an ice-filled glass, garnish with lime rounds if desired, and serve.

SWEET AND FLORAL

Lavandula

Follow the recipe above, replacing the palm sugar syrup with **Lavender Syrup** (page 124) and substituing **Bärehnjäger honey liqueur** for the liquor. If you like a stiffer drink, add **1 ounce gin, vodka, or pisco**.

BLACKBERRY BOUNTY

Bramble

Muddle ¼ **cup fresh blackberries** in a cocktail shaker until broken up and juicy. Proceed with recipe, substituting **1 ounce Chambord** and **1 ounce Averna** for the spirit.

LIGHT AND LIVELY

Cool as a Cucumber

Muddle **1 tablespoon fresh rosemary needles** and **2 English cucumber slices**. Proceed with recipe, substituting **Dill, Cucumber, and Black Peppercorn Vodka** (page 129) for the spirit. Garnish with **rosemary sprigs** and **cucumber slices**.

Rainbow Sherbet Punch

From frat houses to holiday dinner buffets, rainbow sherbet punch has made a gaudy appearance at many a celebration. Its appeal is questionable, but maybe the booze content allows this kitsch concoction to keep on trucking. This version sheds the punch's saccharine reputation while retaining its colorful persona, bringing in fresh flavors from the tropics. Use a brut wine to avoid returning to its overly sweet origins.

1 (750-milliliter) bottle Pineapple Rum (page 130), chilled

2 cups Homemade Sour Mix (page 131)

1 cup Domaine de Canton ginger liqueur

2 cups club soda, chilled

2 (750-milliliter) bottles brut white sparkling wine or brut rosé, chilled

Ice mold (page 10)

3 pints rainbow sherbet, or 3 pints assorted sherbets such as mango, pineapple, and lemon

Stir rum, sour mix, ginger liqueur, and club soda together in a punch or other serving bowl. When ready to serve, stir in sparkling wine and slide in ice mold. Scoop all sherbet into the punch, or scoop individual portions into serving cups and ladle punch over sherbet. Serve immediately.

Sorbet vs. Sherbet

What's the difference between sorbet and sherbet, aside from tricky pronunciation? Dairy. Sherbet has a small amount of it, making it part sorbet (which contains no dairy, just fruit) and part ice cream. The result? Think of a well-balanced mouthful of orange creamsicle.

Sunny Side Up Punch

· MAKES 13 CUPS ·
(ABOUT 3 QUARTS), SERVES 24

This punch has a base of lemonade and sparkling wine, already a bright and refreshing way to mix a bowl of mirth. Add smoky spiced honey and minty shiso-infused liquor, and the recipe takes off on a flavor road trip.

4 cups fresh lemon juice, strained and chilled
1 (750-milliliter) bottle Shiso Gin, Sake, or Vodka (page 130), chilled
2 cups Chile-Spiced Honey Syrup (page 124)
2 (750-milliliter) bottles sparkling wine, chilled
Ice mold (page 10)
3 lemons, sliced into rounds, for garnish

Stir together lemon juice, infused spirit, and syrup in a punch or other serving bowl. When ready to serve, stir in sparkling wine and slide in ice mold. Add lemon rounds and serve immediately.

Freeze Frame

Make easy work of thinly slicing citrus fruits by freezing them for about 15 minutes before taking a knife to them. Always use a sharp chef's knife for smooth, clean cuts.

Moroccan Mint Iced Tea

· MAKES 1 QUART ·

A tall pitcher of iced tea turns down the heat even before you've taken the first sip. Add mint to the equation, and there is no comparison. The gunpowder green tea used here is steeped twice to reduce its bitterness.

6 cups water, divided
2 tablespoons gunpowder green tea pellets
1½ cups fresh mint leaves, plus more for garnish
2 tablespoons Honey Syrup (page 124), or more to taste
Ice
8 ounces vodka, gin, or Black Pepper Gin or Vodka (page 129), chilled, optional
Lemon or lime rounds, for garnish

Bring 1 cup water to a boil over high heat in a medium saucepan. Reduce heat to medium-low and simmer. Add tea pellets and simmer for 1 minute; do not stir or swirl. Strain and set aside the liquid, and return pellets to saucepan.

Add another 1 cup water to saucepan and bring to a simmer, swirling pan to rinse pellets. Strain and discard the liquid and return solids to pan.

Add the remaining 4 cups water and the reserved tea liquid to saucepan and bring to a simmer. Simmer for about 3 minutes, remove from heat, and stir in mint. Let cool to room temperature.

Strain tea into an ice-filled pitcher and discard solids. Stir in honey syrup and liquor, if using. Serve immediately in ice-filled glasses, garnishing with fresh mint and lemon or lime rounds.

Moroccan Mint Iced Tea

Lemonade

· SERVES 1 ·

Pack any of these lemonades into large mason jars or insulated containers and bring them along on a picnic or other outdoor get-together.

2 ounces gin, vodka, white rum, pisco, or dry sake

¼ cup freshly squeezed lemon juice, plus ½ teaspoon finely grated lemon zest

1 tablespoon Honey Syrup (page 124), or more to taste

Pinch salt

Ice cubes

¼ cup club soda, chilled

Lemon rounds, for garnish (optional)

Stir liquor, lemon juice and zest, honey syrup, and salt in an ice-filled shaker for about 30 seconds. Add club soda and stir just to combine. Strain into an ice-filled glass and garnish with lemon rounds, if desired. Serve.

BEAUTIFUL BOUQUET

Basilica

Muddle ¼ **cup fresh basil leaves** in the shaker. Use **Rhubarb and Celery Gin or Vodka** (page 129), and replace sweetener with **Lemongrass-Basil Syrup** (page 124). Garnish with **basil leaves**.

HATS OFF

Raspberry Beret

Muddle ¼ **cup raspberries** in the shaker. Use **Black Peppercorn Gin or Vodka** (page 129), and replace sweetener with **Rose Syrup** (page 124).

FUN AND FLIRTY

The Marty

Fill a glass with alternating ice cubes and **Pickled Cherries and Rhubarb** (page 135). Use **Rhubarb and Celery Gin or Vodka** (page 129), and replace sweetener with **Ginger Syrup** (page 125).

LEADER OF THE PACK

Pink Ladies Lemonade

Place **2 tablespoons Rhubarb Jam** (page 141) in a tall glass and fill with ice and **2 sliced strawberries**. Use **Strawberry Gin or Vodka** (page 130) and sweeten with **Rhubarb Syrup** (page 125). Add **1 to 2 tablespoons Rhubarb-Plum Shrub** (page 127) and garnish with a **rhubarb stalk**.

Pink Ladies Lemonade (left) and the Marty (right)

Peachy Keen Punch

Bourbon, like its fellow brown spirits, is a liquor I normally use to make winter cocktails. Paired with peaches and almonds, however, bourbon is perfect for summer drinks, too. This harmonious trio conjures up freshness, perfume, and smokiness.

½ cup packed dark brown sugar

1 tablespoon finely grated orange zest

8 medium peaches (about 3 pounds), pitted and cut into 8 wedges each

1 (750-milliliter) bottle bourbon, chilled, divided

Pinch salt

2 (750-milliliter) bottles prosecco, chilled

2 cups amaretto or almond liqueur, chilled

1 cup freshly squeezed orange juice, strained and chilled

Ice mold (page 10)

Poach the peaches: Line a baking sheet with parchment paper. Rub sugar and orange zest together until no orange strands remain. Combine peaches, sugar mixture, $1/2$ cup of the bourbon, and salt in a medium saucepan and cook over medium-high heat, gently stirring from time to time, until tender, 6 to 8 minutes. Pour peaches and cooking liquid onto prepared sheet, cover loosely with plastic wrap, and refrigerate until cold, at least 30 minutes.

Make the punch: Combine prosecco, the remaining bourbon, amaretto, and juice in a punch or other serving bowl. Stir in chilled peaches and any accumulated juices. Slide in ice mold and serve immediately, scooping peaches into each glass.

Hawaiian Punch

The point of punch is to mix something potent, set up the bowl in the middle of the room, and walk away—after pouring yourself a cup, of course. This tropical mixture is an all-around favorite. You might consider making two batches.

2 (750-milliliter) bottles dark rum or Pineapple Rum (page 130), chilled

2 cups guava nectar, chilled

2 cups fresh orange juice, strained and chilled

1 cup passion fruit juice, chilled

1 cup fresh lime juice, strained and chilled

½ cup grenadine, or more to taste

2 tablespoons Angostura bitters

Ice mold (page 10)

Ice cubes for serving

Maraschino cherries, for garnish (optional)

Pineapple wedges, for garnish (optional)

Stir together rum, guava nectar, juices, grenadine, and bitters in a punch or other serving bowl. When ready to serve, slide in ice mold. Serve in ice-filled cups and garnish with cherries and pineapple wedges if desired.

Chill Out
Make this punch up to 2 days in advance and keep refrigerated until ready to serve.

Hawaiian Punch

Tickled Pink Punch

Lemonade and its blushing bride, pink lemonade, are summer staples. This punch draws upon the timeless classic but sneaks into the liquor cabinet and dresses up with seasonal items like rhubarb and strawberries.

3 cups fresh lemon juice, strained and chilled

1 (750-milliliter) bottle Strawberry Vodka (page 130), chilled

2 cups Rhubarb Syrup (page 125)

2 (750-milliliter) bottles pink sparkling wine, chilled

Ice mold (page 10)

1 quart strawberries, hulled and sliced, for garnish

3 lemons, sliced into rounds, for garnish

Stir together lemon juice, vodka, and syrup in a punch or other serving bowl. When ready to serve, stir in sparkling wine and slide in ice mold. Garnish with strawberries and lemon rounds and serve immediately.

FROSTY DRINKS

Remember slurping a frigid drink

through a straw when you were a child and seeing stars after the chill hit your brain? Although that's a thrill better left to the kids, it might be a challenge to take it slow with these chilled cocktails, popsicles, and iced desserts—boozy, one and all— made with tropical fruits, ice cream, and bubbly.

MELON GRANITA . . . 81

The Glinda . . . 81

PIÑA COLADA . . . 82

Ginger-Lemongrass Piña Colada . . . 82

Lychee-Lime Piña Colada . . . 82

THE MIDAS . . . 84

THE PENELOPE . . . 85

The Cabana Boy . . . 85

THE LUXE . . . 87

Float Your Boat . . . 87

Chocolate-Cherry Shake . . . 87

AHOGADO . . . 88

RASPBERRY REDUX . . . 90

Hold It . . . 90

HOT WATERMELON SHERBET . . . 93

WATERMELON REFRESHER . . . 94

Green Goddess . . . 94

PEACH MELBA SHAKE . . . 97

PROSECCO-BLUEBERRY-LEMON POPS . . . 98

STRAWBERRY-ELDERFLOWER POPS . . . 100

TEQUILA-AVOCADO-TOMATILLO POPS . . . 101

MANGO-SHISO-SAKE POPS . . . 101

LEMON LOVE . . . 103

Melon Granita

Honeydew and cantaloupe often get a bad rap. I often see people push the pastel orange and green squares to the side of their plate. When you get a good melon, though, you'll appreciate the sweet taste, which has notes of honey. This granita accentuates those flavors with salt, honey syrup, and Strega, an herbal Italian liqueur with hints of saffron, honey, and fennel. Enjoy this alongside Prosciutto and Butter Tartines (page 153).

1 cantaloupe or honeydew melon, cut into 1½-inch cubes

½ cup Honey Syrup (page 124)

2 tablespoons lemon juice

Maldon sea salt, to taste

Freshly cracked black pepper, to taste

16 ounces Strega (2 ounces per ½-cup serving)

Make the granita: Combine melon, syrup, and lemon juice in the bowl of a food processor and process until completely smooth. Season with sea salt and pepper. Transfer mixture to a medium bowl and place in the freezer. Scrape mixture with a fork once every hour until completely frozen.

Scoop granita into dessert cups or bowls and then pour 2 ounces Strega over each serving. Sprinkle with additional pepper, if desired. Serve immediately.

A PRETTY, PRETTY REFRESHMENT

The Glinda

Serve the granita in large wineglasses instead of dessert cups. Pour the Strega and about **2 ounces brut sparkling wine** over each.

Melon Prep

Always scrub melons prior to cutting (they grow directly on soil and require thorough cleaning). Running a knife through a dirty melon will only drag any surface filth into the flesh. For this recipe, trim the skin as you would a pineapple or watermelon (see page 19). Cut the melon in half, and with a soup spoon or ice-cream scoop scrape out and discard the seeds. Cut melon into cubes and proceed with recipe.

Piña Colada

An elaborately garnished drink that looks as if it was concocted by Carmen Miranda, the piña colada is sweet, boozy, and a bit much. This version is a fresh take on the chilly classic: frozen pineapple cubes add tartness and concentrated fruit flavor, and coconut milk replaces cloying cream of coconut, allowing the pineapple to shine through. Don't cheat and use pineapple juice and ice. This is the real deal.

1 cup frozen pineapple cubes

¼ cup unsweetened coconut milk

1½ ounces light rum

1 ounce dark rum

2 tablespoons sweetened
 condensed milk

Fresh pineapple cubes,
 for garnish (optional)

Maraschino cherries, for garnish
 (optional)

Fresh lychees, for garnish
 (optional)

Combine pineapple cubes, coconut milk, both rums, and sweetened condensed milk in a blender. Pulse until smooth. Transfer to a glass and add garnish of your choice.

IF YOU LIKE PIÑA COLADA . . .

Ginger-Lemongrass Piña Colada

Substitute **1¹⁄₂ ounces Ginger Rum** (page 130) for the light rum and add **1 tablespoon grated lemongrass** (page 18) to the blender. Proceed with recipe.

PINEAPPLE OF MY EYE

Lychee-Lime Piña Colada

Add ¹⁄₂ **cup canned lychees** and the **finely grated zest of** ¹⁄₂ **lime** to the blender. Proceed with recipe.

The Midas

· SERVES 1 ·

Frozen fruits are ideal for summer cocktails, adding a chill as well as flavor and color to recipes. Prep pineapple yourself (page 19), or buy it already cubed, and then freeze it in zip-top bags until ready to use. This cocktail is a blend of tart pineapple and creamy coconut with a splash of ginger liqueur that adds an edgy bite at the end.

1½ cups frozen pineapple cubes

2 ounces unsweetened coconut milk

2 ounces Pineapple Rum (page 130)

1 ounce Domaine de Canton ginger liqueur

Simple Syrup (page 123), to taste

Combine pineapple, coconut milk, rum, liqueur, and simple syrup in a blender. Pulse until smooth. Pour into a large glass and serve immediately.

Freezing Pineapple

See page 19 for step-by-step instructions for preparing pineapple. Arrange pineapple cubes on a sheet tray and freeze until solid. Once frozen, store cubes in a zip-top bag for use in cocktails and smoothies. For an extra-boozy layer (and to make the most of your ingredients), cube and freeze the pineapple used to make Pineapple Rum (page 130).

The Penelope

SERVES 1

Chill out with this frosty pineapple drink. Be ready to go by keeping frozen pineapple in stock all summer long.

2 cups frozen pineapple cubes
2 ounces tequila
1 ounce Cointreau
1 ounce fresh lime juice
Simple Syrup (page 123), to taste
Lime wedge, for garnish

Combine pineapple, tequila, Cointreau, lime juice, and simple syrup in a blender. Pulse until smooth. Pour into a large glass, garnish with lime wedge, and serve immediately.

JUST KEEP THEM COMING

The Cabana Boy

Replace the tequila with **bourbon**, the Cointreau with **amaretto**, and the lime juice with **fresh orange juice**.

The Luxe

Dark-skinned cherries are available only for a short time in the summer. When they are fresh, get as many as you can. Eat them raw, bake them into a pie, and definitely whip them into this shake.

1 cup vanilla ice cream

2 to 4 tablespoons milk

1 cup fresh or frozen cherries, pitted, plus more for garnish

2 ounces Luxardo maraschino liqueur

1 ounce Cherry-Vanilla Syrup (page 125), or to taste

In a blender, combine all ingredients. Blend until smooth and pour into a glass. Garnish with additional cherries. Serve immediately.

A SODA FOUNTAIN TREAT

Float Your Boat

Substitute **6 ounces cherry soda** for the milk and syrup.

A MATCH MADE IN HEAVEN

Chocolate-Cherry Shake

Add **2 ounces finely chopped 60 to 70 percent cacao chocolate** before blending.

Ahogado

Ahogado is a Spanish word meaning "drowned," and this drink is inspired by the traditional Italian dessert *affogato*, in which vanilla ice cream is "drowned" in perfectly pulled espresso. Here, chocolate or coffee ice cream is drowned in Kahlúa that is steeped with cinnamon and smoky morita chile. The flavors are reminiscent of spiced Mexican hot chocolate.

2½ ounces Kahlúa

1 morita chile

1 cinnamon stick

½ cup coffee or chocolate ice cream

Place Kahlúa, chile, and cinnamon stick in a small saucepan. Simmer for 2 minutes and then cover and let chile steep until plump, about 10 minutes. (Alternatively, combine these ingredients in a microwavable bowl, microwave for 2 minutes, cover, and let steep until chile is plump.) Remove chile and chop; reserve for garnish. Remove and discard cinnamon stick.

Return Kahlúa to a simmer. Meanwhile, scoop ice cream into a dessert bowl. Pour warm Kahlúa over ice cream and garnish with chopped chiles if desired.

Raspberry Redux

· SERVES 1 ·

Red berries and chocolate are a foolproof combination. Here tart raspberries pop against a backdrop of velvety chocolate ice cream and get an ID-required bonus in the form of black raspberry liqueur.

1 cup chocolate ice cream

2 to 4 tablespoons milk

1 cup fresh raspberries, plus more for garnish

2 ounces Chambord

In a blender, combine all ingredients and blend until smooth. Pour into a glass. Garnish with additional raspberries and serve immediately.

SHAKES FOR THE YOUNG CROWD

Hold It

For this all-ages variation, omit the Chambord. (In fact, all the shakes in this book can be prepared without alcohol.)

Hot Watermelon Sherbet

In this recipe, ripe, refreshing watermelon gets hot and bothered, like the recipient of a smoldering look from across the bar. First it is frozen and whipped with coconut milk and agave nectar, and then the addition of chile-morita-infused Chiquila turns up the temperature.

6 cups frozen seedless watermelon cubes

1 cup unsweetened coconut milk

Finely grated zest and juice of 2 limes

2 tablespoons agave nectar or honey, or more to taste

½ cup Chiquila (page 129)

Pinch salt

Puree all ingredients together in a food processor until smooth. Transfer to a large bowl or plastic container and freeze for 30 to 60 minutes, until firm enough to scoop. (The texture will still be soft; do not expect it to be as firm as ice cream.) Scoop sherbet into dessert cups and serve immediately. Alternatively, pour the pureed mixture into ice pop bags (see page 154 for sources) and freeze.

Cubism

Frozen watermelon cubes make a refreshing snack and a colorful alternative to ice cubes, and they form the base of this sherbet. See the step-by-step process on preparing pineapple (page 19) and follow the same method for trimming the exterior of the watermelon. Cut the watermelon into planks and then into approximately 1½- to 2-inch cubes. Arrange cubes in a single layer on a baking sheet and freeze until solid. If you're saving them for a use other than this recipe, store them in a large zip-top plastic bag.

Watermelon Refresher

Watermelon and cucumber are foods that double as thirst-quenchers, especially when juiced, as in this recipe and its variation. Stir in pisco (a potent grape brandy), lime-inflected cilantro, cool mint, and bright and spicy jalapeño, and you've got the summer heat in a chokehold.

3 tablespoons packed fresh cilantro leaves, plus sprigs for optional garnish

3 tablespoons packed fresh mint leaves, plus more for optional garnish

½ jalapeño pepper, chopped, plus rings for optional garnish

3 tablespoons granulated or raw cane sugar

Salt

1½ cups (about 10 ounces) seedless watermelon cubes

2 ounces pisco

Crushed ice

Muddle cilantro and mint leaves, chopped jalapeño, sugar, and a pinch of salt in a shaker. Reserve 3 watermelon cubes for garnish.

In a blender, pulse the remaining watermelon and pisco until completely pureed. Pour through a cheesecloth-lined strainer or nut milk bag into shaker (discard solids), along with a handful of ice, and shake. Strain into an ice-filled glass and garnish with the reserved watermelon cubes, plus cilantro, jalapeño, and mint, if desired. Serve immediately.

A CUCUMBER ELIXIR

Green Goddess

Replace the watermelon with **1 large Persian cucumber**, cut into ¹/₂-inch dice, and the pisco with **Dill, Cucumber, and Black Peppercorn Gin, Sake, or Vodka** (page 129). Garnish with **sliced cucumber** and **jalapeño rounds**.

Strained Relations

Nut milk bags are made of fine mesh and are used to strain nut particulates when making almond, cashew, and other nut-based milks. They are ideal for straining juices, and, best of all, they are washable and reusable. See page 154 for sources.

Peach Melba Shake

Pêche Melba is an Auguste Escoffier original. The famed French chef and culinary writer created the dessert of peach, raspberry sauce, and vanilla ice cream for Nellie Melba, an Australian opera singer, in the late 1800s. Simple but posh, the dessert remains popular today. Here it takes the form of a spiked milkshake made with poached peaches.

1 cup vanilla ice cream

2 to 4 tablespoons milk

½ cup fresh raspberries, plus more for garnish

8 poached peach wedges (see below), divided

2 ounces crème de cassis

POACHED PEACHES

4 ripe but firm peaches, pitted and cut into 8 wedges each

¾ cup Riesling

½ cup crème de cassis

1 3-inch piece lemon peel

In a blender, combine ice cream, 2 tablespoons of the milk, raspberries, 6 peach wedges, and crème de cassis. Blend until smooth, adding the remaining 2 tablespoons milk as needed to achieve desired consistency. Pour into a glass, stir in raspberries for garnish, and top with the remaining 2 peach wedges. Serve immediately.

To poach the peaches: Combine ingredients in a small saucepan and bring to a boil over medium-high heat. Reduce heat to medium and simmer, stirring occasionally, until peaches are tender and liquid is syrupy, about 5 minutes. Remove from heat and let cool completely. Makes about 3 cups.

Prosecco-Blueberry-Lemon Pops

MAKES 16 (2-OUNCE) POPS

The lilting music emitted from the ice cream truck draws children (and some adults) in a somnambulatory state toward the roving ice chest full of soft-serve, popsicles, and tie-dyed Sno-Cones. The dreamlike trance will ensue after these icy treats made with bubbles and blueberries are enjoyed. Keep them in the freezer for an afternoon delight, or slip them into a glass of crisp prosecco at your next party; they'll add flavor and keep drinks cool.

2 cups fresh blueberries, divided
½ cup Lemon Syrup (page 124)
2 cups prosecco, chilled

Pulse 1 cup of the blueberries, syrup, and prosecco in a blender until blueberries are broken down. Add the remaining 1 cup blueberries and pulse once or twice, just to break them up slightly.

Pour ¼ cup prosecco mixture into each of 16 (3-ounce) disposable cups (such as Dixie brand). Arrange cups on a small sheet tray and place in freezer. Check the pops after 30 minutes; once they begin to freeze, insert pop sticks (if you insert sticks before pops start to firm up, they'll tip over). Freeze until pops are solid.

Let pops sit at room temperature for about 5 minutes and then gently remove them from cups. Serve immediately.

Booze Bags
Ice pop molds abound, so use whichever type you like. Instead of freezing pops on sticks, I like to use ice pop bags, such as Friopop and Zipzicle brands: they require little storage space in cabinets and freezers, and they're disposable—easy to hand out and discard at parties. See page 154 for sources.

Double-Dip
Slip a pop into a chilled glass of bubbly—wide glasses, like stemless wineglasses, work best.

Strawberry-Elderflower Pops

· MAKES 16 (2-OUNCE) POPS ·

The trick to cooking and cocktail making is to balance flavors. Often people puzzle over how to do so, but the answer is simple: see what's in season, on farmers' market tables and in the fields. Think of what people eat in their native regions based on the climate, and you'll easily be able to unlock flavor combinations. These boozy coolers showcase rhubarb and strawberries, which are flush during the summer months. The fizz and florals make them explode on your tongue.

2 cups fresh strawberries, stemmed and hulled

½ cup Rhubarb Syrup (page 125)

2 cups prosecco

2 tablespoons elderflower liqueur

Place strawberries, syrup, prosecco, and elderflower liqueur in a blender and pulse until strawberries are broken down.

Pour ¼ cup of the mixture into each of 16 (3-ounce) disposable cups, such as Dixie brand. Arrange on a small sheet tray and place in freezer. Check the pops after 30 minutes; once they begin to freeze, insert pop sticks (if you insert sticks before pops start to firm up, they'll tip over). Freeze until pops are solid.

Let pops sit at room temperature for about 5 minutes and then gently remove them from cups. Serve immediately.

Hull-ah!

Hulling strawberries may sounds like a complex endeavor, but all you need to do is insert a small paring knife into the top of the strawberry and run it in a circle around the green top, as if you're carving a cone inside. Pluck out and discard the center.

Tequila-Avocado-Tomatillo Pops

Mango-Shiso-Sake Pops

•—— MAKES 12 (2-OUNCE) POPS ——•

•—— MAKES 12 (2-OUNCE) POPS ——•

Creamy avocado freezes into a smooth and velvety ice without the addition of dairy. The tart tomatillos and lime juice gives these popsicles their vibrancy.

Frozen mango cocktails abound but these spiked pops will steal the spotlight. Start with high-quality mango sorbet and stir in infused sake.

4 tomatillos (about 1 pound), husked, scrubbed, and coarsely chopped

½ cup Simple Syrup (page 123) or Lemongrass Syrup (page 124)

1 ripe avocado, pit removed, flesh scooped out

2 teaspoons finely grated lime zest plus ¼ cup fresh lime juice

2 ounces silver tequila

2 tablespoons fresh mint leaves

1 tablespoon fresh cilantro leaves

Pinch salt

3 cups mango sorbet, softened

¾ cup Shiso Sake (page 130)

2 teaspoons finely grated lime zest

Pinch Maldon sea salt

Combine all ingredients in a blender and pulse until mixture is smooth. Pour ¼ cup of the mixture into each of 12 (3-ounce) disposable cups such as Dixie brand or into ice pop bags. Arrange on a small sheet tray and place in freezer. Check the pops after 30 minutes; once they begin to freeze, insert pop sticks (if you insert sticks before pops start to firm up, they'll tip over). Freeze until pops are solid. Let pops sit at room temperature for about 5 minutes and then gently remove them from cups. Serve immediately.

In a medium bowl, stir together all ingredients until combined. Pour ¼ cup of the mixture into each of 12 (3-ounce) cups or into ice pop bags. Arrange on a small sheet tray and place in freezer. Check the pops after 30 minutes; once they begin to freeze, insert pop sticks (if you insert sticks before pops start to firm up, they'll tip over). Freeze until pops are solid. Let pops sit at room temperature for about 5 minutes and then gently remove them from cups. Serve immediately.

Lemon Love

·•· SERVES 1 ·•·

A favorite way to end a summer meal in Italy is with ice-cold limoncello, a tart and sweet lemon liqueur (often homemade according to family recipes) that cleanses the palate and livens the mood. Skip a complicated dessert and instead scoop out good-quality lemon sorbet and douse it with frosty limoncello.

1 scoop lemon sorbet

2 ounces limoncello, chilled

Scoop sorbet into a dessert cup or paper cone and then drizzle with limoncello. Serve immediately.

Lemony Snicket

Eager to make your own limoncello? The premise is simple: steep lemon zest in a neutral spirit until the oils release (it will turn bright yellow), and then mix it with simple syrup. The ratios and density of the syrup change from recipe to recipe. The flavor will be directly affected by the lemons' origin and cultivation as well. Research and test!

ANTIDOTES

A night of rip-roaring debauchery
has a bad habit of sulking when the sun comes up, and even
a demure cocktail can rear its ugly head the morning after it's
been drunk. The antidotes in this section may not be cure-alls,
but you might as well get your hair of the dog, enjoy it,
and try to get on with your day. And, of course, these
cocktails don't require a headache to be consumed.

MIMOSA . . . 107

Mr. Pink . . . 107

SHANDY . . . 108

SANGRITA . . . 110

Tamarind-Oh! . . . 110

CLASSIC BLOODY MARY . . . 113

The Quite Contrary . . . 113

MICHELADA . . . 114

Chelada . . . 114

Rojita . . . 114

Levantamuertos . . . 114

ICED COFFEE . . . 117

SALTY LIME SODA . . . 118

The Cuddly Hudaly . . . 118

Mimosa

SERVES 1

"I'll have a mimosa." The request echoes throughout restaurants every Sunday. Brunch is a revered institution in my book, and a mimosa the only proper way to salute it. Since the two lone ingredients are sparkling wine and orange juice, make sure you have good versions of both. Now is not the time to use the swill you'd sneak into punch or that tinny OJ that's served on airplanes.

2 ounces fresh orange juice, chilled

2 ounces sparkling white wine, chilled

Pour orange juice into a champagne flute and then top with sparkling wine. Serve.

A BLUSHING MIMOSA

Mr. Pink

Replace the orange juice with **fresh grapefruit juice** and add a splash of **crème de cassis**.

Shandy

A shandy, or shandygaff, is a combination of beer and a carbonated beverage such as ginger beer or citrus-flavored soda. I prefer making it with a pale lager or a hefeweizen and strongly flavored ginger beer. In the summer, I add lemony herbs and dried spices like thyme and coriander, which amp up the drink's underlying flavor notes.

1 teaspoon coriander seeds, lightly crushed

1 strip orange zest

1 strip lemon zest

2 rosemary sprigs

4 thyme or lemon thyme sprigs

Ice cubes, if desired

6 ounces beer such as lager or hefeweizen, chilled

4 ounces ginger beer, chilled

Toast coriander seeds in a small skillet over medium-high heat until fragrant, about 1 minute. Transfer to a glass. Carefully run a lit match along orange and lemon zests, rub them on the rim of the glass, and then drop them into glass along with rosemary and thyme. Add ice, if using, and then add beer and ginger beer, stirring gently to combine. Serve.

Sangrita

Salt, lick, shoot, wince. The tequila shot is boorish and sophomoric. Graduate to a tequila that can be sipped and enjoyed alongside *sangrita*, a classic Mexican accompaniment that's savory and spicy and somewhat similar to Bloody Mary mix. In fact, the name means "little blood" or "small blood." Sweeter versions exist, but this one will make your blood come to a heated simmer.

1 teaspoon grated yellow onion

2 tablespoons freshly squeezed lime juice

1 tablespoon freshly squeezed orange juice

Pinch granulated sugar

Salt and freshly ground black pepper to taste

1 tablespoon V8

Hot sauce, to taste

Dash Maggi seasoning sauce or Worcestershire sauce, to taste

In a liquid measuring cup, combine onion, juices, and sugar and let sit for at least 15 minutes. Stir in remaining ingredients and adjust to taste. Serve alongside a 2-ounce shot of tequila.

GRAPEFRUIT AND TAMARIND SANGRITA
Tamarind-Oh!

Reduce the lime juice to 1 tablespoon, and substitute **2 tablespoons freshly squeezed grapefruit juice** for the orange juice. Combine the juices with **1 tablespoon tamarind concentrate**, and stir well to dissolve. Then combine mixture with the onion and sugar and proceed with recipe.

The More, the Merrier

Sangrita can be prepared up to 2 days in advance. If planning to serve a crowd, multiply the recipe and make a pitcher.

Classic Bloody Mary

• SERVES 1 •

Hangovers happen, and cures for them have been peddled and promoted for as long as the perpetrator has existed. Magic cures, potions, rituals—whatever the antidote is purported to be, the Bloody Mary has withstood the test of time as the companion to that morning misery. This version is a stepping stone. Add and subtract condiments to suit your palate and, if you're smart, make a pitcher a day ahead to avoid fumbling for the ingredients in the morning.

SALT RIM

½ lime

2 tablespoons coarse salt, such as Maldon sea salt, crushed

2 teaspoons freshly ground black pepper

1 teaspoon celery salt, optional

COCKTAIL

¾ cup V8, chilled

2 tablespoons clam juice, chilled

2 tablespoons freshly grated horseradish

1 tablespoon lemon juice

1 tablespoon lime juice

2 teaspoons Worcestershire sauce

2 teaspoons hot sauce

2 ounces gin, vodka, or Dill, Cucumber, and Black Peppercorn Gin or Vodka (page 129)

Ice cubes

ACCOMPANIMENTS

Celery stalks

Stuffed olives

1 piece Scallop Ceviche (page 151), skewered

Beer chaser

Classic Bloody Mary with Scallop Ceviche (page 151) garnish

Zest the ½ lime and then cut it in half. In a small saucer, combine salt, pepper, celery salt, and lime zest, rubbing zest into mixture with fingertips. Run a lime wedge along the rim of a chilled highball glass. Dip rim into salt mixture and set glass aside.

In a shaker, stir together all cocktail ingredients to combine. Taste and adjust seasoning as necessary. Fill the prepared highball glass with ice, add drink, and garnish as desired with celery, olives, or scallop skewer. If desired, serve with a beer chaser.

MERRY, MERRY
The Quite Contrary

For the salt rim, omit the celery salt and, optionally, substitute **chile pequín** for the black pepper. Pulse **1 small diced tomatillo** with **2 tablespoons fresh chilled orange juice** and **2 tablespoons lime juice** in a blender until tomatillo is completely blended. Strain into a shaker and stir in **6 tablespoons V8, 2 teaspoons Maggi seasoning sauce or Worcestershire sauce, 2 teaspoons sriracha**, and **2 ounces either sake, Tomatillo and Coriander Tequila** (page 129), **or Chiquila** (page 129). Fill the prepared highball glass with ice, add drink, and garnish with **carrot** and **cucumber** sticks. If desired, serve with a beer chaser.

Michelada

This Mexican-born *antídoto* is served on ice and begins with a base of umami-dense Worcestershire sauce, vinegary hot sauce, and lime juice. A *cubito Maggi,* or bouillon cube, is a popular but optional addition. Suitable for the condiment-shy, the Chelada variation is just as refreshing and reviving as the original. Pickled Shrimp (page 137) makes this drink a more than adequate brunch dish.

2 tablespoons kosher salt

1 teaspoon freshly ground black pepper

½ lime, plus additional lime wedges for garnish

¼ cup fresh lime juice

½ Maggi-brand bouillon cube (optional)

Worcestershire sauce, to taste

Hot sauce, such as Cholula, Valentina, or Tabasco brand, to taste

Crushed ice

1 (12-ounce) bottle pale lager such as Corona, Pacífico, Sol, or Modelo Especial, chilled

Pickled Shrimp (page 137), freshly shucked oysters (page 16), or Scallop Ceviche (page 151), for garnish

Combine salt and pepper on a small plate or saucer. Rub the rim of a chilled 1-pint-capacity glass with lime half to moisten. (Alternatively, pour 1 tablespoon hot sauce onto a small plate and dip rim to coat.) Next, dip rim into salt mixture and shake off excess.

Add lime juice to glass. If using the bouillon, dissolve it in the lime juice. Add Worcestershire and hot sauce and stir with a spoon or cocktail stirrer. Add ice and pour in beer to fill. Gently stir. Garnish as desired, and serve with remaining beer to refill as needed.

PLAN B
Chelada
Replace the salt with **celery salt** and omit bouillon, hot sauce, and Worcestershire sauce.

DIFFERENT SPICE, BUT STILL REAL NICE
Rojita
Replace the hot sauce with **sriracha** and add **2 ounces tomato juice or V8** to the glass. If you're feeling bold, sneak in **a 2-ounce shot of Chiquila** (page 129).

POTENT ENOUGH TO RAISE THE DEAD
Levantamuertos
Add **2 ounces Mint, Cilantro, and Serrano Tequila** (page 129) and **2 ounces Clamato** to the glass. Serve with a **freshly shucked oyster** (page 16).

Iced Coffee

A hangover's most distinguishing symptom is thirst. For this, the best antidotes are water, soda, electrolytes, more water, juice, hair of the dog cocktails—naturally—and, for the caffeine lovers, iced coffee. No hot coffee for me during the summer, thank you. Use lots of ice and, if you like, a splash of booze to help you get on with your day.

1 cup freshly brewed strong
  coffee, cooled

Brown sugar or Simple Syrup
  (page 123), to taste

Milk, half-and-half, heavy cream,
  or sweetened condensed milk,
  to taste

2 ounces Baileys or Kahlúa,
  if desired

Ice

Stir together coffee, sugar or syrup, milk, and liquor (if using) in a tall glass. Add ice and stir to chill. Serve immediately.

Salty Lime Soda

Most of the fruit juices I try are too sweet for my taste. Tropical and citrus juices that should be thirst quenchers instead taste overpowering. But these limeades, cut with salt and smoky curry leaves, are fresh and tart, hydrating to the nth power.

6 fresh curry leaves

2 kafir lime leaves, cut into thin ribbons

2 tablespoons granulated sugar

½ teaspoon salt

¼ cup fresh lime juice

2 ounces white rum

Ice cubes

¼ cup club soda, chilled

Toast curry leaves in a dry skillet over medium heat until fragrant and dry, shaking pan often, about 2 to 3 minutes. Transfer to a shaker. Add lime leaves, sugar, and salt and muddle. Add lime juice, rum, and ice and shake vigorously. Strain into an ice-filled glass and top with club soda. Serve.

A SUAVE AND DANDY DRINK

The Cuddly Hudaly

Replace the white rum with **Tomatillo and Coriander Tequila** (page 129) and the sugar with **1 ounce Honey Syrup** (page 124).

UNDERPINNINGS

Although cocktail making should be a casual affair, high-quality and fresh ingredients are always essential. Underpinnings also deserve careful attention; think of them as the appropriate undergarments for your outfit. This section includes infused liquors that may be enjoyed on their own or mixed into drinks, as well as bar mixes, flavored syrups, and vinegary shrubs. Make your cocktails stand out.

SIMPLE SYRUP . . . 123
Honey Syrup . . . 124
Chile-Spiced Honey Syrup . . . 124
Lavender or Rose Syrup . . . 124
Lemon, Lime, or Grapefruit Syrup . . . 124
Lemongrass Syrup . . . 124
Lemongrass-Basil Syrup . . . 124
Ginger Syrup . . . 125
Mint Syrup . . . 125
Basil, Cilantro, or Dill Syrup . . . 125
Rhubarb Syrup . . . 125
Cherry-Vanilla Syrup . . . 125
SHRUBS . . . 126
Blackberry-Basil Shrub . . . 127
Blueberry-Lemon Shrub . . . 127
Mango Shrub . . . 127
Raspberry Shrub . . . 127
Rhubarb-Plum Shrub . . . 127
Strawberry-Rosemary Shrub . . . 127

INFUSED LIQUORS . . . 128
Mint, Cilantro, and Serrano Tequila . . . 129
Serrano and Lime Tequila . . . 129
Jalapeño, Mint, and Cilantro Tequila . . . 129
Tomatillo and Coriander Tequila . . . 129
Chiquila . . . 129
Dill, Cucumber, and Black Peppercorn Gin,
    Sake, or Vodka . . . 129
Black Peppercorn Gin or Vodka . . . 129
Rhubarb and Celery Gin, Sake, or Vodka . . . 129
Blackberry Gin, Pisco, or Vodka . . . 130
Strawberry Gin or Vodka . . . 130
Shiso Gin, Sake, or Vodka . . . 130
Shiso and Shishito Pepper Gin, Sake, or Vodka . . . 130
Ginger Rum . . . 130
Pineapple Rum . . . 130
HOMEMADE SOUR MIX . . . 131
Lime Sour Mix . . . 131
Orange Sour Mix . . . 131
Grapefruit Sour Mix . . . 131

Simple Syrup

Syrups are made specifically for chilled drinks, because sugar alone, when added to cold liquid, will only settle at the bottom of a glass without adding sweetness. The following syrups can gently sweeten beverages and incorporate layers of additional flavor or contrast. Ratios for ingredients vary according to the desired thickness of the final product, but I prefer a one-to-one sugar-to-water ratio, which yields pourable, easy-to-dissolve syrup. Follow the basic rules and create unique versions of your own. Use the syrups in virgin beverages like lemonade, iced tea, and club soda and, of course, in cocktails such as the Lazarus (page 51) and Moroccan Mint Iced Tea (page 70).

1 cup granulated sugar*
1 cup water

For a richer syrup with a molasses backbone, replace the granulated sugar with demerara or light brown sugar. For a syrup that's robust and mature, replace the granulated sugar with palm sugar. Palm sugar is thick and sweet, almost resembling sugar cookie dough. It is available at many ethnic markets.

Combine sugar and water in a small saucepan. Bring to a boil over medium-high heat, then reduce heat to medium and cook, stirring, until sugar is completely dissolved. Let syrup cool to room temperature and store, refrigerated, in an airtight container for up to 1 month.

For variations, see pages 124 and 125.

SOME SUNSHINE IN YOUR CUP
Honey Syrup

Substitute **1 cup clover or orange blossom honey** for the sugar. Proceed with recipe.

Buzzed

For a mellow honey flavor that won't interfere with delicate and bright flavors, I prefer to use varieties like clover and orange blossom. Buckwheat honey is more pungent, with notes of malt and molasses, and is a bit intense; it works well in robust drinks like the Honey Badger (page 45).

SMOKY, SPICY, SWEET
Chile-Spiced Honey Syrup

Replace sugar with **1 cup buckwheat honey** and add **3 morita chiles** to the saucepan. Continue with recipe on page 123. Once syrup cools, strain and discard chiles.

FLOWER POWER
Lavender or Rose Syrup

Add ½ **cup dried edible lavender flowers or dried edible rosebuds** to the saucepan. Continue with recipe. Once syrup cools, strain and discard solids. This variation makes about 1½ cups.

Bloomers

Dried edible lavender flowers and rosebuds can be purchased online or at specialty markets. Store the dried buds in a zip-top bag or airtight container in a cool, dry place. See page 154 for sources.

ZINGERS
Lemon, Lime, or Grapefruit Syrup

Pulse the sugar with **2 tablespoons finely grated lemon, lime, or grapefruit zest** in a food processor until sugar is damp and no zest strands remain. Alternatively, rub zest into sugar with fingertips. Reduce the water to ½ cup and combine it with the sugar mixture and ½ **cup lemon, lime, or grapefruit juice** in a small saucepan. Continue with recipe on page 123.

Pucker Up

Citrus fruit rinds have natural oils that can add even more kick to drinks and foods. Pulsing or rubbing the zest into sugar (or salt, in savory recipes) is an effective method for releasing these oils.

LIGHT AND LIVELY
Lemongrass Syrup

Pulse **3 lemongrass stalks**, chopped (see page 18), with the sugar in a food processor until sugar is damp and lemongrass is completely broken down. Combine sugar mixture with the water and continue with recipe on page 123, straining and discarding solids when syrup is cool.

SUMMER HERB GARDEN
Lemongrass-Basil Syrup

Follow the directions for Lemongrass Syrup, but add **1 cup fresh basil leaves** to the syrup while it cools.

GINGE-A NINJA
Ginger Syrup

Follow the directions for Lemongrass Syrup, but substitute **1 (6-inch) piece fresh ginger**, thinly sliced, for the lemongrass.

HERBAL ESSENCES
Mint Syrup

After the sugar is completely dissolved, add **2 cups fresh mint,** lightly crushing the leaves, and stir. Continue with recipe, straining and discarding solids when syrup has cooled.

SECRET GARDEN
Basil, Cilantro, or Dill Syrup

Follow the directions for Mint Syrup, but substitute **fresh basil, cilantro, or dill** for the mint.

TART AND TANGY
Rhubarb Syrup

In a small saucepan combine the sugar and water with **2 rhubarb stalks**, trimmed of ends and cut into $1/2$-inch-thick slices, and **1 (1-inch) piece fresh ginger**, peeled and thinly sliced. Bring to a boil over medium-high heat, reduce heat to medium, and cook, stirring, until sugar is completely dissolved and rhubarb is soft, about 10 minutes. Let syrup cool to room temperature, strain, and discard solids. Store syrup, refrigerated, in an airtight container for up to 1 month.

SODA FOUNTAIN REVIVAL
Cherry-Vanilla Syrup

Pulse **3 cups pitted fresh or frozen cherries (about 18 ounces), 1 cup demerara or granulated sugar**, and the **seeds from 2 vanilla bean pods** in a food processor until cherries are completely broken down. Combine mixture with **1 cup water** in a saucepan and bring to a boil over medium-high heat. Reduce heat to medium and cook, stirring, until sugar is completely dissolved. Let syrup cool to room temperature, strain, and discard solids. Stir in **1 tablespoon fresh lemon juice**. Store syrup, refrigerated, in an airtight container for up to 1 month.

Magic Beans

Whole vanilla bean pods should have the texture of soft leather. Use a paring knife to flatten the pod and then slit it in half lengthwise. Run the dull edge of the knife along the interior of each half to scrape out the beans. Then, if you'd like, store the scraped pods in sugar to be used for coffee, tea, or baking: the sugar will be gently infused with vanilla flavor.

Shrubs

Originally, shrubs were acidulated fruit liqueurs once popular in England, but the term also refers to fruit-flavored, sweetened vinegars that were popularized as drinks in colonial times in the United States. The following recipe is what I found to be among the most straightforward and effective in releasing flavor. Experiment with your own combinations!

Use the shrubs to flavor club sodas and sparkling waters as well as aperitifs and cocktails like the Revolver (page 43). For a quick and distinctive aperitif, pour 1 tablespoon of any of these shrubs into a glass of chilled champagne. Shrubs also make a great base for vinaigrettes.

1 cup fruit
1 cup granulated sugar
1 cup vinegar

Prepare the fruit: If using berries, wash them and discard leaves and stems. For fruits with large seeds and tough or inedible skins, such as mangoes, peel, seed, and dice the flesh. Fruits like plums can be sliced or cubed, while stalks like rhubarb should be sliced crosswise. Herbs need merely to be washed, dried, and lightly crushed.

In a medium bowl, combine fruit, herbs (if using), and sugar, mashing and stirring to coat completely. Transfer mixture to a 1-pint or 1-quart jar with a lid. Let fruit macerate for about 20 minutes and then add vinegar. Seal jar and shake vigorously.

Let sit in a cool, dark place or the refrigerator for 3 to 5 days, shaking jar occasionally to redistribute contents. Taste the shrub after the first day and either use or let rest longer. Prior to using, strain and discard solids.

Capture Summer
Prepare shrubs throughout the season. Store them in the refrigerator, and use them for drinks (alcoholic and virgin) year-round.

SHRUBBERY
Blackberry-Basil Shrub
Follow the instructions using **fresh blackberries**, **1/2 cup packed basil leaves**, and **champagne vinegar**.

LITTLE BOY BLUE
Blueberry-Lemon Shrub
Follow the instructions using **fresh blueberries**, **1 teaspoon finely grated lemon zest**, and **white balsamic vinegar**.

MANGO A-GO-GO
Mango Shrub
Follow the instructions using **1 mango**, peeled, pitted, and diced, and **distilled white vinegar**.

RAZZMATAZZ
Raspberry Shrub
Follow the instructions using **fresh raspberries** and **red wine vinegar**.

PLUM PERFECT
Rhubarb-Plum Shrub
Follow the instructions using **2 stalks rhubarb**, sliced crosswise, **1 plum**, pitted and diced, **1/2 cup packed mint leaves**, and **champagne vinegar**.

STRAWBERRY FIELDS
Strawberry-Rosemary Shrub
Follow the instructions using **fresh strawberries**, hulled and sliced, **2 large sprigs rosemary**, coarsely chopped, and **white balsamic vinegar**.

Infused Liquors

Spirits come in countless varieties and flavors, many based on secret recipes. The recipes on pages 129 and 130 are intended to give you a hand in crafting your own cocktail, starting with clean spirits that provide a fairly blank canvas. Start with these suggestions, and then elaborate and expand on your own experiments.

Refer to the steps in the following variations, and then proceed with these additional steps: Place flavoring ingredients in a 1-quart airtight glass jar or other lidded container. Pour in spirit, close tightly, and shake. Store in a cool, dry place; the refrigerator is ideal, especially if using delicate herbs like dill and cilantro, which can easily lose their attractive green hue.

Shake 2 to 3 times per day to redistribute ingredients. Taste the infusion every day; it is ready when the desired flavor intensity has been reached, anywhere between 1 and 5 days.

Strain the infusion through a fine-mesh sieve into a clean vessel; discard any solids. Use a funnel to return infusion to its original bottle. Infused liquor will keep indefinitely, but you may want to smell and taste it before using it in a cocktail if more than 6 months have passed since you made it.

GREEN WITH ENVY

Mint, Cilantro, and Serrano Tequila

Infuse **1 (750-milliliter) bottle silver tequila** with **1 bunch cilantro**, **1 bunch mint**, and **3 serrano chiles**, halved lengthwise. Follow the instructions on page 128.

FEEL THE HEAT

Serrano and Lime Tequila

Infuse **1 (750-milliliter) bottle silver tequila** with **3 serrano chiles**, halved lengthwise, and **3 limes**, quartered. Follow the instructions on page 128.

GO GREEN

Jalapeño, Mint, and Cilantro Tequila

Infuse **1 (750-milliliter) bottle silver tequila** with **1 bunch cilantro**, **1 bunch mint**, and **2 jalapeños**, halved lengthwise. Follow the instructions on page 128.

Serranos vs. Jalapeños

Serrano chiles are bright green, slender, tapered peppers approximately 2 inches in length. Jalapeños are larger, fuller, and darker green and their heat is milder. If you prefer your infusions and your prepared dishes to be less spicy, remove the ribs and seeds from the chiles before proceeding with the recipe.

CURIOUSER AND CURIOUSER

Tomatillo and Coriander Tequila

Infuse **1 (750-milliliter) bottle silver tequila** with **8 tomatillos**, husked and cut into large cubes; **1 tablespoon toasted coriander seeds**; and **2 limes**, zested and quartered. Follow the instructions on page 128.

How to Toast Whole Spices

Always toast whole spices prior to using them in a recipe to release their flavor. Place them in a dry skillet and cook over medium heat, swirling or stirring constantly, until fragrant, 1 to 2 minutes. Immediately remove from heat. Crush spices lightly in a mortar and pestle or with the flat side of a meat tenderizer.

A BURNING, BURNING YEARNING

Chiquila

Infuse **1 (750-milliliter) bottle silver or gold tequila** with **3 morita chiles**. Follow the instructions on page 128.

THE NEW GARDEN SALAD

Dill, Cucumber, and Black Peppercorn Gin, Sake, or Vodka

Infuse **1 (750-milliliter) bottle gin, sake, or vodka** with **¼ cup toasted black peppercorns**, **1 bunch dill** trimmed of stalky ends, and **1 medium English cucumber**, sliced. Follow the instructions on page 128.

CRACK IT

Black Peppercorn Gin or Vodka

Infuse **1 (750-milliliter) bottle gin or vodka** with **¼ cup toasted black peppercorns**. Follow the instructions on page 128.

STALKER

Rhubarb and Celery Gin, Sake, or Vodka

Infuse **1 (750-milliliter) bottle gin or vodka** with **2 rhubarb stalks** and **2 celery stalks**, all sliced crosswise. Follow the instructions on page 128.

BLACKOUT
Blackberry Gin, Pisco, or Vodka
Infuse **1 (750-milliliter) bottle gin, pisco, or vodka** with **3 cups blackberries**. Follow the instructions on page 128.

BERRY NICE
Strawberry Gin or Vodka
Infuse **1 (750-milliliter) bottle gin or vodka** with **3 cups strawberries**, hulled and sliced. Follow the instructions on page 128.

SHISO COOL
Shiso Gin, Sake, or Vodka
Infuse **1 (750-milliliter) bottle gin or vodka or 750 milliliters dry sake** with **12 shiso leaves**, thinly sliced. Follow the instructions on page 128.

TRY SAYING IT THREE TIMES
Shiso and Shishito Pepper Gin, Sake, or Vodka
Infuse **1 (750-milliliter) bottle gin or vodka or 750 milliliters dry sake** with **12 shiso leaves**, thinly sliced, and **8 shishito peppers**, halved lengthwise. Follow the instructions on page 128.

About Shiso
This pointy-edged, somewhat bumpy and fuzzy green leaf you may have noticed garnishing sushi platters is in fact completely edible. Shiso, or perilla, tastes like a blend of basil, mint, and citrus. (There is a red variety as well, with a different flavor profile. Use the green in these recipes.) Shiso is available at Japanese markets. If you can't find it on your own, ask a staff member at a Japanese restaurant for shopping suggestions.

A THREE-HOUR TOUR
Ginger Rum
Infuse **1 (750-milliliter) bottle light or golden rum** with **1 (6-inch) piece ginger**, thinly sliced. Follow the instructions on page 128.

YO, HO, HO
Pineapple Rum
Infuse **1 (750-milliliter) bottle light or golden rum** with **1 small pineapple**, peeled, cored, and cubed (see page 19 for prep tips). Follow the instructions on page 128.

Store Your Boozy Pineapple
Unlike the solids used in the other infusions, which should be discarded when the infusion is done, pineapple can be reused to make cocktails. After straining the infusion, reserve the pineapple cubes. Arrange them in a single layer on a sheet tray and freeze until solid, and then store them in a zip-top bag in the freezer until needed. Your cocktail will get a one-two punch.

Homemade Sour Mix

Mass-produced sour mix, or bar mix, is sold by the gallon, and though it's a convenient solution, the neon-green concoction is sugary sweet and lacks the sour punch that fresh citrus delivers. Making the mix at home is no great feat, and it keeps for up to a month. Your cocktails will be transformed.

1 cup granulated sugar

3 tablespoons finely grated lemon zest

3 tablespoons finely grated lime zest

1 cup water

1 cup fresh lemon juice (from about 8 lemons), strained

1 cup fresh lime juice (from about 12 limes), strained

Pulse sugar and zests in a food processor until sugar is damp and no zest strands remain. Alternatively, rub zests into sugar with fingertips. Combine sugar mixture and water in a medium saucepan and cook over medium heat, stirring, until sugar is completely dissolved. Let syrup cool to room temperature and then stir in juices. Refrigerate in an airtight container for up to 1 month. Shake before using.

IN THE LIMELIGHT

Lime Sour Mix

Increase lime juice to $1\frac{1}{2}$ cups and decrease lemon juice to $\frac{1}{2}$ cup.

ORANGE YOU GLAD

Orange Sour Mix

Replace lime zest with **orange zest** and substitute **$1\frac{1}{2}$ cups fresh orange juice** for the lime juice. Decrease lemon juice to $\frac{1}{2}$ cup.

GROVE FOR IT

Grapefruit Sour Mix

Replace lime zest with **grapefruit zest** and substitute **$1\frac{1}{2}$ cups fresh grapefruit juice** for the lime juice. Decrease lemon juice to $\frac{1}{2}$ cup.

FILL YOUR PLATE

Though some might opt for liquid repasts, a full belly is a more advisable way to carry on. Plus, entertaining is not really entertaining when guests are given nothing to nibble but swizzle sticks, olive pits, and fingernails. The recipes here range from pickled vegetables perfect for garnishing and snacking to heartier offerings that will satiate even the most ravenous appetites, like fried chicken, buttermilk biscuits, and bacon-wrapped hot dogs covered in guacamole.

PICKLED CHERRIES AND RHUBARB . . . 135

Pickled Rhubarb . . . 135

Pickled Okra and Radishes . . . 135

PICKLED SHRIMP . . . 136

FRIED CHICKEN . . . 138

BUTTERMILK BISCUITS . . . 140

RHUBARB JAM . . . 141

CHARRED SHISHITO PEPPERS . . . 141

SLIDERS . . . 142

Lamb Sliders . . . 142

Pork Sliders . . . 143

DOWNTOWN L.A. DOGS WITH GUACAMOLE . . . 144

CHILE, CHORIZO, AND POTATO BREAKFAST TACOS . . . 147

YOGURT-MARINATED CHICKEN KEBABS . . . 148

PEANUT MASALA . . . 150

SCALLOP CEVICHE . . . 151

PROSCUITTO AND BUTTER TARTINES . . . 153

Fig and Ricotta Tartines . . . 153

Tuna Niçoise Tartines . . . 153

Pickled Cherries and Rhubarb

· MAKES 1 QUART ·

Although proper pickles and jams can keep for months, these recipes are made for instant gratification. You can enjoy them as soon as they're cold! Serve them alongside Fried Chicken (page 138) or, for an unexpected use, add them to drinks such as the Marty (page 73). See page 17 for more on the quick pickling process.

2½ cups fresh cherries, pitted

3 stalks rhubarb, cut crosswise into ¼-inch-thick slices

1-inch piece ginger, peeled and thinly sliced

1 teaspoon black peppercorns

½ teaspoon whole cloves

½ teaspoon whole allspice

2 cups red wine vinegar

½ cup granulated sugar

½ teaspoon salt

Place cherries, rhubarb, and ginger in a 1-quart vessel, such as a mason jar. Line a small bowl with a roughly 6-inch square of cheesecloth.

Toast peppercorns, cloves, and allspice in a dry medium saucepan over medium-high heat until fragrant, about 1 minute. Pour spices into prepared bowl and tie cheesecloth into a bundle.

Combine vinegar, sugar, and salt in saucepan and stir over medium-high heat until sugar is completely dissolved. Add spice bundle and bring to a boil. Add bundle to cherries and rhubarb and, with a funnel, pour hot liquid into jar. Cover and refrigerate until contents are cool, at least 2 hours. Refrigerate pickles, covered, for up to 1 week.

LOVE IT OR LEAVE IT

Pickled Rhubarb

Replace cherries with **additional rhubarb**. Use it to add crunch and a tart bite to salads or serve alongside macaroni and cheese.

SAVORY GARNISHES

Pickled Okra and Radishes

Replace the red wine vinegar with **white vinegar** and the cherries and rhubarb with **8 okra**, halved lengthwise, and **1 bunch (about 2 cups) radishes**, thinly sliced. Add **2 peeled garlic cloves** and **1 bay leaf**. Continue with recipe, but leave jar uncovered while the mixture cools in the refrigerator (okra tends to produce a funny smell). You may omit the okra and pickle radishes alone; these pair perfectly with the Gibson (page 38). Carrots, pearl onions, zucchini, squash, and any other crisp vegetable also work well.

Pickled Shrimp

Leave shrimp cocktail at the steakhouse this summer and try this pickled version, instead. Serve them as finger food and use them to garnish cocktails, especially antidotes. See page 17 for more on the quick pickling process.

1 tablespoon black peppercorns

2 teaspoons coriander seeds

½ cup distilled white vinegar

¼ cup water

½ teaspoon salt

8 garlic cloves

¼ cup fresh lime juice

1 tablespoon white tequila

24 to 30 large peeled, deveined, and cooked shrimp (tails on if possible)

4 serrano chiles, halved lengthwise

12 kaffir lime leaves*

4 fresh curry leaves**

*Kaffir limes are highly fragrant. Both the fruit and leaves may be purchased at specialty markets. See page 154 for sources. Store leaves in zip-top bags in the freezer.

**Fresh curry leaves are deep green and have a smoky, toasty, and savory taste. See Sources (page 154) for vendors.

Clockwise from top left: Pickled Okra and Radishes (page 135), Pickled Cherries and Rhubarb (page 135), olives with cheese, Pickled Shrimp, oysters and Sangrita (page 110), and Scallop Ceviche (page 151)

In a dry small saucepan, toast peppercorns and coriander seeds over medium heat until fragrant, about 1 minute. Add vinegar, water, salt, and garlic. Bring to a boil over medium-high heat and cook for 5 minutes. Remove from heat and let cool to room temperature. Stir in lime juice and tequila.

Pack shrimp, serranos, kaffir lime leaves, and curry leaves into a 1-quart jar with a lid. Pour in vinegar mixture, adding water if needed to fully submerge shrimp. Seal jar and refrigerate for at least 8 hours and up to overnight prior to serving.

Serve as a hors d'oeuvres with saltine crackers or use to garnish a Michelada (page 114) or Classic Bloody Mary (page 113). Shrimp should be eaten within 2 days of preparation.

Fried Chicken

SERVES 4

Fried chicken conjures Southern hospitality, picnics, and summer gatherings. This recipe, which can be easily doubled for large parties, uses tangy buttermilk as an adherent for a seasoned flour dredge. The secret to a crisp coating is to double dip the chicken, and the key to juicy meat is using boneless, skinless thighs. Pair with fluffy biscuits (page 140) covered with butter.

4 bone-in, skin-on chicken thighs

Salt and freshly ground black pepper

4 to 6 cups peanut or vegetable oil

1½ cups buttermilk

1 teaspoon finely grated lemon zest

1 tablespoon lemon juice

2 cups all-purpose flour

1½ teaspoons garlic powder

1½ teaspoons onion powder

1 teaspoon paprika

1 teaspoon dried thyme

¼ teaspoon cayenne pepper

Set a cooling rack on a large rimmed baking sheet or over paper towels. Line a work surface with parchment paper or plastic wrap.

Using a paper towel for easy handling, remove and discard the chicken skin. Run the tip of a paring knife closely along the bone of each thigh to remove it from the meat. Trim and discard any excess fat. Season both sides of each thigh with salt and pepper.

Heat oil in a large high-sided skillet to 350°F. In a medium bowl, whisk together buttermilk, lemon zest, and lemon juice.

In a pie plate or on a dinner plate, stir together flour, garlic powder, onion powder, ½ teaspoon salt, 1 teaspoon black pepper, paprika, thyme, and cayenne with a fork.

One at a time, dip each chicken thigh into buttermilk with one hand. Place chicken in flour mixture and, using the other hand, dredge meat and shake off excess. Transfer to the prepared work surface. Repeat with remaining thighs, and then dip and dredge each piece a second time.

Fry chicken, in batches if necessary to avoid crowding in the pan, and check the temperature of the oil every so often with an instant-read thermometer; if temperature drops, let it return to 350°F before adding the next batch. Cook chicken for 4 to 5 minutes per side, or until an instant-read thermometer reads 165°F when inserted into the thickest part of the meat. With tongs, transfer chicken to prepared cooling rack.

When all chicken is cooked, sprinkle chicken with salt, if desired, and serve immediately or at room temperature. Refrigerate leftovers.

Buttermilk Biscuits

MAKES 12 (2½-INCH) BISCUITS

I've been testing biscuit recipes since I was eight years old. I have childhood notebooks smattered with notes on what worked and what didn't. These biscuits are the ones I've been making for a good ten years. Light, layered, and inordinately tall, they're perfection. For an even lighter biscuit, replace half the all-purpose flour with cake flour. Always eat these straight from the oven with a generous slathering of good butter.

3 cups all-purpose flour,
  plus more for dusting

1 tablespoon baking powder

1 tablespoon granulated sugar

1½ teaspoons salt

½ teaspoon baking soda

1 stick (4 ounces) unsalted butter,
  cut into thin slices and chilled

1½ cups buttermilk, chilled, divided

Salted butter, at room temperature,
  for serving

Place oven rack in the middle position and preheat oven to 425°F. Line a large rimmed baking sheet with parchment paper. In a large bowl, whisk together flour, baking powder, sugar, salt, and baking soda. Using two dinner knives, cut butter into flour mixture. Alternatively, quickly work butter into flour mixture by coating the butter pieces with flour and running them through your thumb and ring finger as if you were snapping your fingers. Butter should be in pea-size pieces.

Fold in 1 cup of the buttermilk with a rubber spatula. If the mixture looks dry, add more buttermilk, 1 tablespoon at a time. Turn out dough onto a lightly floured surface and knead just until dough is cohesive. Pat dough into a 10-inch rectangle and fold into thirds. Repeat procedure twice more and then pat into a 1-inch-thick circle.

Flour a 2½-inch round biscuit cutter or the rim of a glass of similar circumference and cut out biscuits. Arrange them about ½ inch apart on prepared baking sheet. Bake until fluffy and golden, 12 to 15 minutes, and then transfer to a cooling rack. Serve warm.

Ring the Dinner Bell

Round out the menu: Serve fried chicken and biscuits with Pickled Cherries and Rhubarb (page 135) and a simple salad of bitter greens or kale sautéed in a bit of oil and garlic. Rhubarb Jam (page 141) is an irresistible spread on these biscuits.

Rhubarb Jam

· MAKES 2 CUPS ·

This pink jam is easy to make and matches perfectly with Buttermilk Biscuits (page 140), but it also takes an unexpected role in one of the Lemonade variations (page 73). Raw rhubarb is intensely tart, but a bit of sugar transforms it.

8 rhubarb stalks (about 1 pound), ends trimmed and cut crosswise into ¼-inch slices
1 cup granulated sugar
1 teaspoon finely grated lemon zest
2 tablespoons lemon juice
1 tablespoon water
Pinch salt

Combine all ingredients in a medium saucepan and bring to a boil over medium-high heat. Reduce heat to medium and simmer, stirring occasionally, until rhubarb has completely broken down, 12 to 15 minutes. Remove from heat and let cool to room temperature. Serve immediately or store, refrigerated, in an airtight container. Jam will keep for up to 2 weeks.

Get to Know Rhubarb

Rhubarb is a vegetable with long stalks that are rubbery and fibrous, similar to celery. Its leaves are large and resemble rainbow chard. You'll recognize rhubarb by its color, grading from pale green to carnation pink to ruby red. Bracing and bitter when raw, it makes a surprising addition to salads. Cooked with sugar, it breaks down into sweet jam and melts into summer pies.

Charred Shishito Peppers

· SERVES 4 AS AN APPETIZER ·

Shishitos are mild Japanese peppers, green and fingerlike in their slenderness. They are delicious when sautéed and can be served as an appetizer or as a side to cocktails like the Flavor Flav (page 37). They also can be used as flavoring agents in alcoholic infusions (pages 128–130).

1 tablespoon vegetable oil
8 ounces shishito peppers*
Maldon or coarse sea salt, to taste

Heat oil in a large skillet over medium-high heat until shimmering. Add peppers and cook, tossing and stirring occasionally, until blackened in some spots. Transfer to a platter and season with salt. Serve immediately.

Shishito peppers are available at Japanese markets and often at farmers' markets. Padrón peppers are an acceptable substitute.

Sliders

The burger is king of the grill, but palates have ventured far beyond the traditional beef cheeseburger. Here are some good ways to change it up.

1 tablespoon vegetable oil

1 small onion, finely chopped

1 garlic clove, finely chopped

½ teaspoon garlic powder

½ teaspoon onion powder

1 slice white bread, such as pullman loaf, torn into small pieces

⅓ cup whole milk

1½ pounds ground beef

1 teaspoon salt

½ teaspoon freshly ground black pepper

8 small dinner rolls or slider buns

8 slices yellow or white American cheese

Garnishes such as sliced white onion rounds, sliced tomatoes, iceberg lettuce, and pickle chips

Condiments such as ketchup, mayonnaise, mustard, etc.

Heat oil in a small skillet over medium-high heat until shimmering. Add onion, garlic, garlic powder, and onion powder and cook, stirring, until softened, about 3 minutes. Transfer to a large bowl. Add bread and milk and blend together with a fork until mixture forms a paste. Add beef, salt, and pepper and combine with your hands.

With clean, damp hands, separate beef into 8 portions and shape each into a 3-inch round patty. Gently press a finger into the center to create a divot.

Heat grill to medium-high, or lightly brush a large skillet with vegetable oil and place over medium-high heat. Cook burgers to desired doneness, about 2 to 3 minutes per side for rare and 4 to 5 minutes per side for well done.

Arrange patties on a platter and serve alongside buns, garnishes, and condiments.

FEELING SHEEPISH

Lamb Sliders

Replace ground beef with **ground lamb**. Omit garlic powder and onion powder. Add **1 tablespoon fresh mint**, chopped, **1 tablespoon fresh flat-leaf parsley**, chopped, and **2 tablespoons chopped red onion** to meat mixture before shaping. Proceed with recipe. To serve, combine 1½ **cups full- or low-fat Greek yogurt** with **2 tablespoons chopped fresh dill, 1 minced garlic clove, 1 tablespoon lemon juice,** and salt and pepper to taste; spoon over burgers and serve on buns or in **warm folded pita bread.** If desired, make gremolata: combine **2 tablespoons chopped flat-leaf parsley** and **2 tablespoons grated lemon zest,** and then stir in **2 finely chopped garlic cloves.** Serve with sliders.

PIG OUT
Pork Sliders
Replace ground beef with **ground pork** (fattier cuts like shoulder or country-style pork ribs will make patties that are juicy and rich). Proceed with recipe. For serving: Heat **2 tablespoons unsalted butter** in a small saucepan over medium-high heat until bubbling. Add **2 cups chopped peaches** and **2 tablespoons dark brown sugar.** Cook, stirring, until heated through and caramelized, about 3 minutes. Scoop over burger patties and serve with **spicy mustard** and **small onion rolls.**

Downtown L.A. Dogs with Guacamole

· MAKES 8 HOT DOGS ·

Move over, ballpark franks heated in swampy water! These deluxe hot dogs are wrapped in bacon and buried under fresh guacamole and caramelized chiles and onions. Serve these dogs with your favorite hot sauce (I like Valentina and Cholula brands), pickled carrots, and jalapeños for even more heat.

½ cup cornstarch

8 hot dogs

8 strips bacon

4 ripe but firm avocados, pitted, peeled, and cut into ½-inch dice

Juice of 2 limes

1 tablespoon cider vinegar

2 cups tightly packed cilantro leaves, chopped

Heat a grill or large cast-iron skillet over medium-high heat.

Scatter cornstarch on a dinner plate. Roll each hot dog in cornstarch, shaking off excess. Wrap each hot dog in a strip of bacon (the cornstarch will make the bacon adhere); set aside.

To make the guacamole: Lightly mash avocados in a medium bowl with a fork—some chunks should remain. Add lime juice, vinegar, cilantro, mint, minced white onion, garlic, and tomato and gently stir to combine. Season to taste with salt and pepper; set aside.

½ cup mint leaves, finely chopped

½ cup minced white onion

2 garlic cloves, minced

1 ripe beefsteak tomato, seeded and coarsely chopped

Salt and freshly ground black pepper

6 jalapeño peppers, seeds and ribs removed

1 large Vidalia onion, peeled and cut into 8 wedges

¼ cup vegetable oil

½ cup mayonnaise

8 hot dog buns

Brush jalapeños and Vidalia onion wedges with oil and grill until charred. Set aside to cool. Lightly oil grill or skillet and arrange hot dogs in a single layer. Cook until bacon is cooked through and lightly charred, turning with tongs as necessary.

Chop 2 of the charred jalapeños and half the onion wedges and stir into guacamole. To serve, spread the inside of hot dog buns with mayonnaise, tuck hot dogs in buns, and top with guacamole. Serve with the remaining charred jalapeños and onion wedges, along with any other desired condiments and garnishes.

Chile, Chorizo, and Potato Breakfast Tacos

· MAKES 4 TACOS ·

These breakfast tacos are inspired by southern California street food and Mexican ingredients. Neither the chorizo nor the poblano chiles are overly spicy—just warm enough to tease the tongue. Tortillas charred on an open flame acquire a smoky, flaky exterior, and potatoes sautéed in chorizo fat will crisp on the outside. Always scramble eggs over low heat for tender, rather than rubbery, results. Serve these with Micheladas (page 114).

1 cup cilantro leaves, chopped

½ cup white onion, chopped

1 large poblano chile

8 large eggs

Salt and freshly ground black pepper

2 medium Red Bliss or Yukon Gold potatoes

1 tablespoon plus 2 teaspoons vegetable oil, divided

6 ounces chorizo, crumbled or finely chopped

1 garlic clove, minced

8 small (6-inch) corn tortillas, plus more if desired, warmed over an open flame, or in a dry skillet, and wrapped in a clean kitchen towel

Lime wedges, for serving

Sliced radishes, for serving

Hot sauce, for serving

Combine cilantro and onion in a serving bowl; set aside.

Cook poblano over an open flame or in a dry skillet over high heat until completely blackened. Wrap in foil and set aside for 10 minutes or until cool enough to handle. Wipe off charred skin with paper towel. Remove and discard stem and finely chop.

Crack eggs into a medium bowl and whisk in salt and pepper; set aside.

Cut potatoes into ½-inch dice. Place in a medium microwave-safe bowl and drizzle with 1 tablespoon oil. Season with salt and pepper and cover tightly with plastic wrap. Microwave for about 6 minutes, until fork-tender. (Alternatively, place potatoes in a medium saucepan, cover with cold water, and add 1 tablespoon salt. Bring to a boil over medium-high heat, then reduce heat to medium and simmer until fork-tender. Drain.)

Heat 2 teaspoons oil in a large skillet over medium-high heat until beginning to smoke. Cook chorizo until browned; transfer to a plate. Add potatoes to skillet and cook, stirring occasionally, until browned, about 5 minutes. Add garlic and cook until fragrant, about 30 seconds. Immediately return chorizo and poblanos to skillet and stir to combine.

Reduce heat to medium-low, add eggs, and cook, stirring constantly with a heat-proof rubber spatula for small curds and evenly cooked eggs. Scoop each serving of eggs on two stacked tortillas and garnish with cilantro and onion. Serve with lime wedges, radishes, and hot sauce.

Yogurt-Marinated Chicken Kebabs

SERVES 4 TO 6

This Indian-influenced dish cooks quickly, is perfect for the grill, and is packed with bright, smoky, and spicy flavors that appeal to a wide range of palates. Serve it with Peanut Masala (page 150) or with rice pilaf well freckled with herbs.

2 tablespoons vegetable oil, plus more for grilling

10 fresh curry leaves

5 garlic cloves, minced

1 tablespoon sweet paprika

1 tablespoon garam masala

2 teaspoons ground cumin

2 teaspoons finely grated lemon zest

1 teaspoon finely grated lime zest

1½ cups full-fat Greek yogurt

1 tablespoon fresh lemon juice

1 tablespoon fresh lime juice

2 pounds boneless, skinless chicken breasts cut into 1½- to 2-inch cubes

Salt and freshly ground black pepper

Heat oil in a small saucepan over medium heat until shimmering. Add curry leaves, garlic, paprika, garam masala, cumin, and lemon and lime zests and cook, stirring, until spices and garlic are fragrant and curry leaves are toasted, 3 to 4 minutes. Transfer to a large mixing bowl and whisk in yogurt and lemon and lime juices.

Season chicken with salt and pepper and stir into yogurt-spice mixture. Refrigerate chicken and allow to marinate for 1 to 2 hours.

Heat grill to high heat and brush with oil. Skewer chicken on metal or wooden skewers (if using wooden, presoak in water for 15 minutes to avoid charring). Grill kebabs until chicken is marked with grill lines and cooked through, about 15 minutes. Serve.

Peanut Masala (top; see page 150) and Yogurt-Marinated Chicken Kebabs

Peanut Masala

This is one of my favorite appetizers from India. With meaty peanuts, crunchy bits of pappadam (lentil or chickpea chips), red onion, bright herbs, and a heavy dose of spices, the dish hits multiple flavor notes and textures. Tortilla chips may be easier to find than pappadam and provide the same crunch while blending seamlessly with the other ingredients; feel free to substitute them. Try this dish with Yogurt-Marinated Chicken Kebabs (page 148), or serve it as a side dish with pork, chicken, or seafood tacos.

1 tablespoon vegetable oil

2 tablespoons garam masala*

1 teaspoon ground cumin

4 cups salted cocktail peanuts

1 tablespoon fresh lime juice

3 cups salted pappadam or tortilla chips, crushed

1 medium red onion, finely chopped (about 1 cup)

1 cup packed cilantro leaves, chopped

2 jalapeño peppers, seeds and ribs removed, chopped

Garam masala is a blend of spices containing turmeric, black pepper, cinnamon, cumin, and cardamom. You can make your own to balance the flavors to your liking. Toast the spices in a dry skillet over medium heat for about 1 minute, tossing constantly, and then transfer to a mortar and pestle or a spice mill and grind.

Heat oil over medium heat in a large skillet and add garam masala and cumin. Cook to "bloom" the spices (making them more flavorful), about 30 seconds. Add peanuts and stir to coat evenly. Transfer to a large bowl and add lime juice, tossing to combine. Add remaining ingredients and serve.

Scallop Ceviche

Ceviche is marinated raw fish and/or shellfish. People often think of it as being uncooked, but in fact acids alter, or denature, protein in the same manner as heat, so when prepared correctly ceviche is perfectly safe to eat. You'll notice the translucent fish becoming opaque upon contact with citrus or other acids. I recommend marinating the scallops in this recipe for 15 to 20 minutes; you can increase the time to as long as 30 minutes, but the flesh will become firmer and more rubbery as the clock ticks. Note that thinner and smaller pieces of fish will absorb the marinade more quickly. These scallops are a great pairing with the Classic Bloody Mary (page 113).

12 sea scallops, tough side muscle removed

Salt and freshly ground black pepper

1 teaspoon finely grated orange zest

¼ cup fresh orange juice

1 teaspoon finely grated lime zest

¼ cup fresh lime juice

2 teaspoons extra-virgin olive oil

¼ medium red onion, finely chopped or sliced

1 jalapeño pepper, ribs and seeds removed, finely chopped

Season scallops with salt and pepper. In a medium bowl, whisk together remaining ingredients. Add scallops, toss to coat evenly, cover with plastic wrap, and refrigerate for 15 to 20 minutes. Serve immediately.

Fishy Business

Buy fish from a trusted source, and ask when the fish was delivered. Keep fish on ice until the moment you begin preparing it. Ask the fishmonger for a bag of ice for transportation, and, once at home, arrange the fish on top of an ice-filled tray or ice packs, cover with plastic wrap, and cover with more ice.

When buying scallops, ask for dry packed, if available. Wet-packed scallops are soaked in a phosphate solution, which keeps them looking white but also bloats them with water; this means you'll pay for water weight, and the scallops won't brown properly during cooking. If using wet-packed scallops, rinse them and thoroughly pat dry before using.

The side muscle is a meaty, rubbery nub attached to the scallop that is rather chewy. Remove it before cooking or marinating.

Prosciutto and Butter Tartines

· SERVES 4 ·

These open-faced sandwiches are unfussy but beautiful and hearty; they can be served as full meals or cut up and passed around like hors d'oeuvres. Always start with good sturdy bread, like ciabatta or rustic boule, and use toppings that echo the season and place: fresh goat cheese, ripe figs, sweet tomatoes, herbs from the garden. Try both sweet and savory accompaniments. If entertaining a crowd, set up a table with toppings, cheeses, spreads, fruits, and vegetables so that guests can make their own.

4 thick slices crusty bread, such as boule or ciabatta

6 tablespoons good-quality butter, at room temperature

Maldon or other flaky sea salt and freshly ground black pepper

¼ pound prosciutto, sliced

Spread each slice of bread with butter and season with salt and pepper. Top with prosciutto and serve.

WORTH A FIG

Fig and Ricotta Tartines

Spread **4 thick slices crusty bread** generously with **½ to 1 cup fresh full-fat ricotta or 4 ounces goat cheese** and top with **8 ripe figs,** sliced or quartered (two pieces per slice of bread). Drizzle each with **honey** to taste, season with salt and pepper, and top with a few **oregano leaves** and, if desired, **8 good-quality anchovy fillets,** either salt- or oil-packed (two per slice).

A BIG FISH

Tuna Niçoise Tartines

Brush ¼ **cup olive oil** onto both sides of **4 thick slices crusty bread** and then grill or broil until lightly charred. Top them with **1 cup good-quality tuna packed in olive oil; 2 hard-boiled eggs,** chopped; **1 cup cherry or grape tomatoes,** halved; and ½ **cup basil leaves,** thinly sliced. Drizzle sandwiches with **juice of 1 lemon** and season with **salt and pepper.** Garnish with ½ **cup caperberries.**

SOURCES

AMAZON
Friopop and Zipzicle brand disposable bags for frosty treats.
www.amazon.com

ANTHROPOLOGIE
Serveware, barware, and housewares.
www.anthropologie.com

COCKTAIL KINGDOM
All things bar related, from ice trays and tongs to bitters and syrups.
www.cocktailkingdom.com

CRATE AND BARREL
Serveware, barware, and cookware.
www.crateandbarrel.com

KALUSTYAN'S
Specialty international market carrying every dry good and spice you can imagine, and then some.
www.kalustyans.com

MEXGROCER
Specialty Latin American products.
www.mexgrocer.com

POTTERY BARN
Serveware, barware, and cookware.
www.potterybarn.com

SUR LA TABLE
Kitchen supplies galore, including barware and serveware.
www.surlatable.com

TOVOLO
King-size and "perfect" square silicone ice cube trays, orb-shaped ice molds, ice pop molds, and other kitchen tools.
www.tovolo.com

WEST ELM
Serveware, barware, and housewares.
www.westelm.com

WILLIAMS-SONOMA
Kitchen supplies, cookware, barware, serveware, and housewares.
www.williams-sonoma.com

INDEX

a

affogato, 88
Ahogado, 88
almond liqueur, *see* amaretto
amaretto, 43, 45, 74, 85
Amaretto Sour, 45
Aperol, 59
Arroz con Mango, 34
Asti Spumante, 64
As You Like It, 37
Averna, 51, 67

b

Badda Bang!, 40
Badda Bing, The, 40
Baileys, 117
Bärenjäger, 23, 67
Basilica, 73
Basil Syrup, 125
beer, 108, 113, 114
biscuits, buttermilk, 140
Blackberry-Basil Shrub, 43, 127
Blackberry Gin, Pisco, or Vodka,
   44, 130
Black Peppercorn Gin or Vodka, 51, 70,
   73, 129
Bloody Mary, 113
Blueberry-Lemon Shrub, 127
Bollywood Margarita, 56
bourbon
   Badda Bang!, 40
   Cabana Boy, The, 85
   Honey Badger, 45
   Kentucky Mule, 26
   Mint Julep, 32
   Peachy Keen Punch, 74
   Professor Plum, 44
   Whitney's Lollipop, 23
Bramble, 67
brandy, 63
Bumby, The, 40
Butler, The, 44
Buttermilk Biscuits, 140

c

Cabana Boy, The, 85
Campari
   Bumby, The, 40
   Italian Greyhound, 46
   Negroni, 49
   Negroni Vampiro, 49
   Playa, The, 27
   Sourpuss, 45
   Whitney's Lollipop, 23
ceviche, 151
Chambord, 27, 67, 90
Champagne
   Bee Sting, 23
   Butler, The, 44
   Honey Badger, The, 45
   La Rosita, 51
   Negroni Sbagliato, 49, 51
   Poison, The, 43
Charred Shishito Peppers, 37, 141
Chartreuse, 46
Chelada, 114
Cherry Pop, 24
Cherry-Vanilla Syrup, 24, 40, 87, 125
Chile, Chorizo, and Potato Breakfast
   Tacos, 147
Chile-Spiced Honey Syrup, 45, 70, 124
Chino-Latino, 34
Chiquila
   Hot Watermelon Sherbet, 93
   Margarita, 56
   Pulparindo, 30
   Quite Contrary, The, 113
   recipe, 129
   Rojita, 114
Chiquila Mockingbird Margarita, 56
Chocolate-Cherry Shake, 87
Cilantro Syrup, 125
Classic Bloody Mary, 113
Cocchi Americano, 40, 46, 48, 49
coffee liqueur, *see* Kahlúa
Cointreau, 29, 46, 56, 85
Cool as a Cucumber, 67

crème de cassis, 27, 97, 107
Cuba Libre, 24
Cuddly Hudaly, The, 118

d

Dagger, The, 44
Daiquirí, 40
Dark and Stormy, 46
Dill, Cucumber, and Black Peppercorn
   Gin, Sake, or Vodka, 37, 67, 94, 113,
   129
Dill Syrup, 125
Dolce Far Niente, 63
Domaine de Canton, 68, 84
Downtown L.A. Dogs with
   Guacamole, 144
Drambuie, 45
Dubonnet, 48

e

elderflower liqueur, 43, 100
El Papa Doble, 40

f

Fig and Ricotta Tartines, 153
Flavor Flav, 37
Float Your Boat, 87
Fresco de Arroz con Piña, 34
Fried Chicken, 138
frizzante, *see* Lambrusco
fruit cup, 54

g

Gibson, 39
gin
   Blackberry Gin, 130
   Black Peppercorn Gin, 129
   Classic Bloody Mary, 113
   Dill, Cucumber, and Black
      Peppercorn Gin, 129
   Gibson, 39
   Lemonade, 73
   Limeade, 67

Long Island Iced Tea, 29
Martini and variations, 37
Morrocan Mint Iced Tea, 70
Negroni and variations, 49
Playa, The, 27
Rhubarb and Celery Gin, 129
Shiso and Shishito Pepper Gin, 130
Shiso Gin, 130
Strawberry Gin, 130
ginger liqueur, *see* Domaine de Canton
Ginger-Lemongrass Piña Colada, 82
Ginger Rum, 33, 34, 82, 130
Ginger Syrup, 73, 125
glassware, 13
Glinda, The, 81
granita, 81
Grapefruit Sour Mix, 131
Grapefruit Syrup, 124
Green Goddess, 94
Greyhound, 46

h

Hawaiian Punch, 77
Hold It, 90
Homemade Sour Mix
    Dolce Far Niente, 63
    La Dolce Vita, 64
    Long Island Iced Tea, 29
    Rainbow Sherbet Punch, 68
    recipe, 131
    Sourpuss, 45
Honey Badger, 45
honey liqueur, *see* Bärenjäger
Honey Syrup
    Chiquila Mockingbird
        Margarita, 56
    Cuddly Hudaly, 118
    Glinda, The, 81
    Lemonade, 73
    Melon Granita, 81
    Moroccan Mint Iced Tea, 70
    recipe, 124
hot dogs, 144
Hot Watermelon Sherbet, 93

i

Iced Coffee, 117
iced tea, 70. *See also* Long Island
    Iced Tea
ice pops, 98, 100, 101
Infused Liquors, 128
In the Parlor, 43
Italian Greyhound, 46

j

Jalapeño, Mint, and Cilantro
    Tequila, 129
julep, 32

k

Kahlúa, 88, 117
kebabs, chicken, 148
Kentucky Mule, 26

l

La Dolce Vita, 64
Lambrusco, 63
Lamb Sliders, 142
La Rosita, 51
Lavandula, 67
Lavender Syrup, 51, 67, 124
La Vie en Rose, 51
Lazarus, The, 51
Lemonade, 73
lemongrass, how to prepare, 18
Lemongrass-Basil Syrup, 73, 124
Lemongrass Syrup, 101, 124
Lemon Love, 103
Lemon Syrup, 124
Levantamuertos, 114
Lillet, 37, 49
Limeade, 67
lime soda, salty, 118
Lime Sour Mix, 56, 131
Lime Syrup, 124
limoncello, 103
Long Island Iced Tea, 27
Love-Love, 55
Lucky Loser, 54
Luxardo, *see* maraschino liqueur
Luxe, The, 87
Lychee-Lime Piña Colada, 82

m

Mango-Shiso-Sake Pops, 101
Mango Shrub, 34, 44, 127
maraschino liqueur, 40, 87
Margarita, 56
Marimar, The, 37
Martini, 37
Marty, The, 73
Matchpoint, 54
Melon Granita, 81
Michelada, 114
Midas, The, 84
milkshake, 87, 90, 97
Mimosa, 107
Mint, Cilantro, and Serrano Tequila,
    114, 129
Mint Julep, 32
Mint Syrup, 125
Morrocan Mint Iced Tea, 70
Moscow Mule, 26
Mr. Pink, 107

n

Negroni, 49
Negroni Sbagliato, 49
Negroni Vampiro, 49
Nigel Barker, The, 46

o

Orange Sour Mix, 131
oysters, how to shuck, 16

p

pantry and fridge basics, 8–9
Peach Melba Shake, 97
peach schnapps, 27
Peachy Keen Punch, 74
Peanut Masala, 150
Penelope, The, 85
Pickled Cherries, 40, 135
Pickled Cherries and Rhubarb, 73, 135
Pickled Okra and Radishes, 135
Pickled Rhubarb, 135
Pickled Shrimp, 114, 137
pickles, quick, 17
Pimm's Editions, 54
Piña Colada, 82
Piñata, 31

pineapple, how to prepare, 19, 130
Pineapple Rum, 27, 68, 76, 84, 130
Pink Ladies Lemonade, 73
pisco
    Blackberry Pisco, 130
    Lemonade, 73
    Limeade, 67
    Piscola, 24
    Trouble in Paradisi, 59
    Watermelon Refresher, 94
Piscola, 24
Playa, The, 27
Poison, The, 43
Pork Sliders, 143
Professor Plum, 44
Prosciutto and Butter Tartines, 153
prosecco, 23, 43, 74, 98, 100
Prosecco-Blueberry-Lemon Pops, 98
Pulparindo, 30
punch, 62–77

q

Queen of Hearts, 48
quick pickles, how to make, 17
Quite Contrary, The, 113

r

Rainbow Sherbet Punch, 68
Raspberry Beret, 73
raspberry liqueur, see Chambord
Raspberry Redux, 90
Raspberry Shrub, 44, 127
Revolver, The, 43
Rhubarb and Celery Gin, Sake,
   or Vodka, 37, 73, 129
Rhubarb Jam, 73, 141
Rhubarb-Plum Shrub, 44, 73, 127
Rhubarb Syrup, 73, 77, 100, 125
Rojita, 114
rosé, 51, 68
Rose Syrup, 51, 73, 124
rum
    Cuba Libre, 24
    Dagger, The, 44
    Daiquirí, 40
    Dark and Stormy, 46
    Ginger Rum, 130
    Hawaiian Punch, 77

Lemonade, 73
Limeade, 67
Long Island Iced Tea, 29
Piña Colada and variations, 82
Pineapple Rum, 130
Salty Lime Soda, 118
South of the Border, 33
rum and coke, 24
Rum and Soda, 24
rye whiskey, 40

s

sake
    Chino-Latino, 34
    Dill, Cucumber, and Black
      Peppercorn Sake, 129
    Lemonade, 73
    Limeade, 67
    Quite Contrary, The, 113
    Rhubarb and Celery Sake, 129
    Sake to Me, 52
    Shiso Sake, 130
    Shiso and Shishito Sake, 130
Sake to Me, 52
Salty Dog, 46
Salty Lime Soda, 118
sandwiches, open-faced, 153
sangría, 63, 64
Sangrita, 110
Scallop Ceviche, 113, 114, 151
Serrano and Lime Tequila, 129
Sex on the Beach, 27
Shandy, 108
sherbet, 93
sherbet punch, 68
Shirley Temple, 23
Shiso and Shishito Pepper Gin, Sake,
   or Vodka, 37, 130
Shiso Gin, Sake, or Vodka, 70, 101, 130
Shrub Cocktails, 43–44
Shrubs, 126
Simple Syrup
    Daiquirí, 40
    Fresco de Arroz con Piña, 34
    Iced Coffee, 117
    Limeade and variations, 67
    Midas, The, 84
    Mint Julep and variation, 32

Penelope, The, and variation, 85
Pimm's Editions and variations, 54
Pulparindo and variation, 30
    recipe, 123
Sake to Me, 52
Tequila-Avocado-Tomatillo
    Pops, 101
Sliders, 142
sour mix, 131
Sourpuss, 45
South of the Border, 32
sparkling wine
    Bee Sting, 23
    Glinda, The, 81
    Honey Badger, 45
    La Vie en Rose, 51
    Mimosa, 107
    Poison, The, 43
    Rainbow Sherbet Punch, 68
    Sunny Side Up Punch, 70
    Tickled Pink Punch, 77
    See also Asti Spumante, Champagne,
      Lambrusco, prosecco
St-Germain, see elderflower liqueur
stocking your bar, 14–15
Strawberry-Elderflower Pops, 100
Strawberry Gin or Vodka, 55, 73, 77, 130
Strawberry-Rosemary Shrub, 43, 54,
   127
Strega, 81
Sunny Side Up Punch, 70

t

tacos, breakfast, 147
Tamarind-Oh!, 110
tartines, 153
tequila
    Chiquila, 129
    Jalapeño, Mint, and Cilantro
      Tequila, 129
    La Vie en Rose, 101
    Long Island Iced Tea, 29
    Margarita, 56
    Mint, Cilantro, and Serrano
      Tequila, 129
    Penelope, The, 85
    Pickled Shrimp, 137
    Serrano and Lime Tequila, 129

Tomatillo and Coriander Tequila, 129

Tequila-Avocado-Tomatillo Pops, 101

Tickled Pink Punch, 77

tools and serveware, 10–12

Tomatillo and Coriander Tequila, 56, 113, 117, 129

triple sec, 29, 56

Trouble in Paradisi, 59

Tuna Niçoise Tartines, 153

v

vermouth, 37, 39, 43, 49

vodka

Blackberry Vodka, 130

Black Peppercorn Vodka, 129

Classic Bloody Mary, 113

Dill, Cucumber, and Black Peppercorn Vodka, 129

Lemonade, 73

Limeade, 67

Long Island Iced Tea, 29

Moroccan Mint Iced Tea, 70

Moscow Mule, 26

Nigel Barker, The, and variations, 46

Playa, The, and variation, 27

Rhubarb and Celery Vodka, 129

Shiso and Shishito Pepper Vodka, 130

Shiso Vodka, 130

Strawberry Vodka, 130

w

Watermelon Refresher, 94

white wine, 51, 97

Whitney's Lollipop, 23

wine spritzer, 51

y

Yogurt-Marinated Chicken Kebabs, 148

ACKNOWLEDGMENTS

A SECOND BOOK SEEMED LIKE AN EASY TASK, BUT IT WAS JUST AS MUCH EFFORT as the first. It was a different process but a welcome one. When I was conceptualizing the recipes and visuals, the summer theme allowed me to think and taste in Technicolor. I love the recipes in this book, and the images that accompany them are fabulous. For that I thank Tara Striano, talented photographer, funny lady, and brave soul, for working with me. Thank you, glorious prop stylists Penelope Bouklas and Emily Rickard: your taste and style is evident in each of these photos. Geraldine Pierson, Eric Martz, Jessica O'Brien, Florencia Azpiroz, Ari Bekian: friends and kitchen-slash-mental support, thank you.

Thank you to all who cheered on the book—and me—throughout the writing: my *mami*, María Argüello, best friend, best mom, best woman; *a mi papá*, José Cuadra Chamorro, *por su cariño y apoyo*; José Alejandro Cuadra, Chiquitín, Natalie Fey, Juan Carlos Cuadra, Whitney Pollett, and Eugenio. Lucky me to have you as my family. Thank you, aunts, uncles, and cousins. Dearest friends John-Paul Doyle, Meghan Erwin, Judith Vanessa Pasos, Sheri Giblin, Lucinda Muise: this book is also for you.
—*María del Mar*

THANK YOU TO OUR AMAZING CREW OF TALENTED INDIVIDUALS WHO WORKED ON the production of the book and helped us make it such a lovely body of work. The company, jokes, lack of sleep, long days, summer heat, YouTube videos, cocktails, and great food really made this book shoot an unforgettable experience. Penelope and Emily, our prop stylists: I am so grateful that we were able to join forces with you both once again on our second cocktails book. You are both amazing stylists. Gee, Ari, Florencia, and Jessica: Thank you all so much. You really worked your butts off on this project. Thank god for those Salty Lime Sodas! Thank you to Ari and Martin at the Wheelhouse (thewheel-housemattituck.tumblr.com) for letting us use your home as one of our locations. It was a perfect fit for the book. To my incredible husband, Eric: You are the best cheerleader a girl could ask for. I love you, babe. Mom: Thank you for being there for me all these years. I love you more than you know. Quirk Books: Thank you so much for making this book happen. Miss Maria: We put a lot of hard work into this book, and once again we created a real beauty. All the laughs, drinks, and fabulous food throughout the process remind me why I love working with you so much. You are an amazing lady. Love you!! —*Tara*

WE WOULD LIKE TO EXTEND SPECIAL THANKS TO OUR SPONSORS AND SUPPORTERS, who provided us with beautiful props and flowers that fleshed out these images and spirits that lifted our own during the production of the book, and, of course, were incorporated into the recipes: Pelligrini Vineyards, LI Spirits, Mattituck Florist, and White Flower Farm House.

ABOUT THE AUTHOR AND PHOTOGRAPHER

A graduate of the International Culinary Center (formerly French Culinary Institute), **MARÍA DEL MAR SACASA** is a food stylist, writer, and consultant who has worked for *Lucky, Vogue,* and *America's Test Kitchen.* Her styling work has appeared in print publications, TV commercials, product packaging, and cookbooks. She lives in New York City and Los Angeles.

TARA STRIANO is a native New Yorker and graduate of NYU. Her photography has been featured in various publications such as *House Beautiful, People, Redbook,* and *Lonny.*

Together, María del Mar and Tara share recipes, photos, and stories from their lives behind the scenes of the food industry on their blog *Cookin' and Shootin'* (www.cookinandshootin.com). This is their second book together.